SIR JOHN SOANE'S MUSEUM

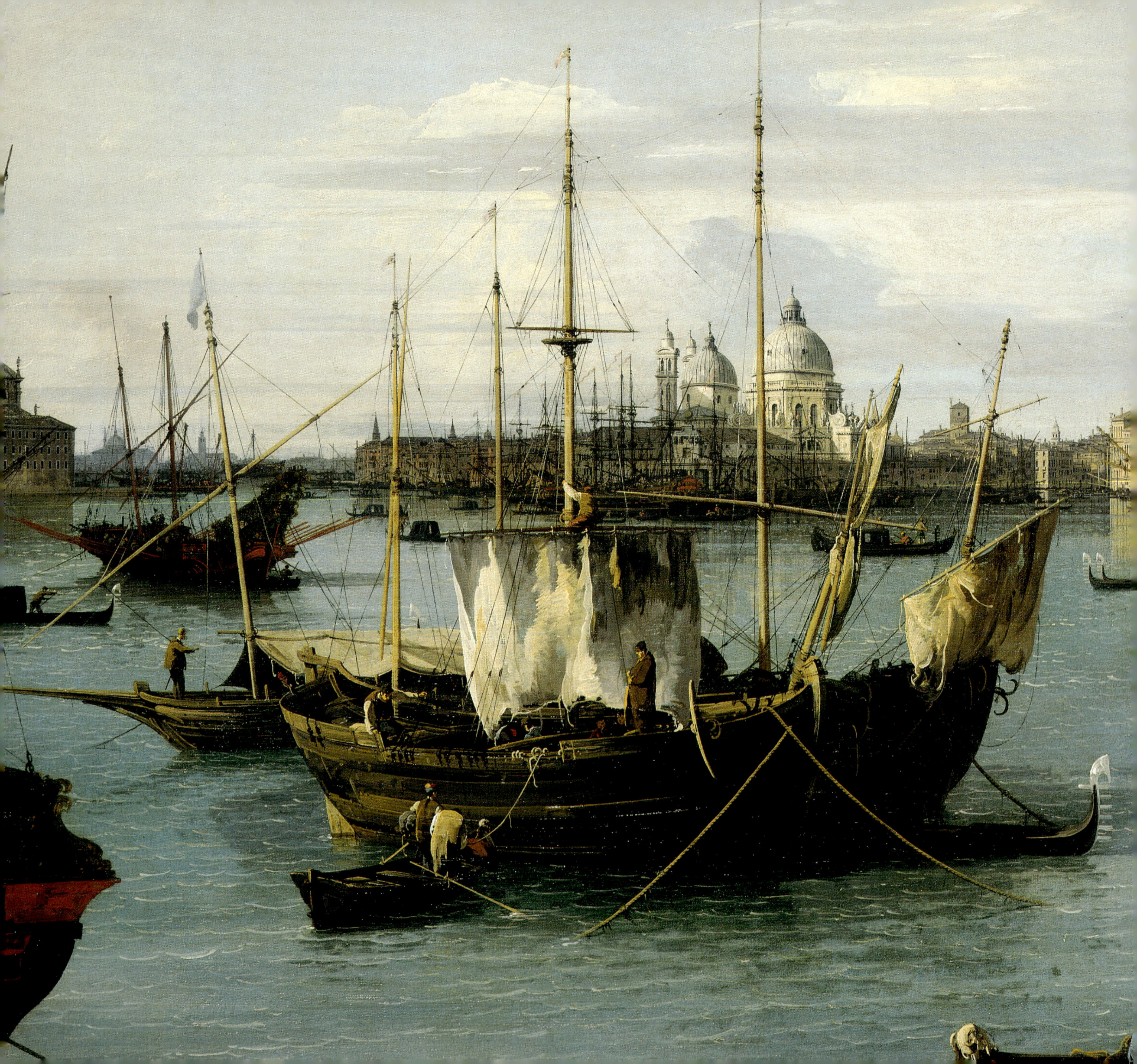

THE SOANE CANALETTOS

J.G. Links

æ
SJSM

Published in the United Kingdom
by Azimuth Editions

Azimuth Editions
33 Ladbroke Grove, London W11 3AY, England
Design by Anikst Associates

British Library Cataloguing in Publication Data
(data applied for)
ISBN 1-898592-14-4

Typeset by Anikst Associates and Azimuth Editions
Printed by PJ Reproductions, London

COVER AND FRONTISPIECE. Details from *The Riva degli Schiavoni, looking West* (PL.1)

Foreword

The publication of this book was made possible by a generous donation from the HEADLEY TRUST

Joe Links died on 1 October 1997, before the final editing of this book for publication. He had, however, completed the text and selected all the images and would, I know, be delighted with the final production which has been overseen by Helen Dorey, our Deputy Curator; as he always said, this is the only picture book to cover three Canalettos in such detail.

The Museum has greatly benefited from Joe's advice and scholarship. When I first re-introduced him to the great *Riva degli Schiavoni* in 1985, he was immediately horrified that it had become so dirty and insisted that we ask Viola Pemberton-Pigott, the Senior Conservator to the Royal Collection, to clean all three Canaletto paintings at the Soane. This she did in 1992–4, and the result has been a revelation of the qualities of paint and light which Joe describes so well in this book.

This is in effect his last work: it is a pleasure to read his words and to hear him guiding us through the Venice depicted in these fine Canalettos – the *Riva* particularly, which always had pride of place in Soane's collection.

Margaret Richardson
Curator, Sir John Soane's Museum

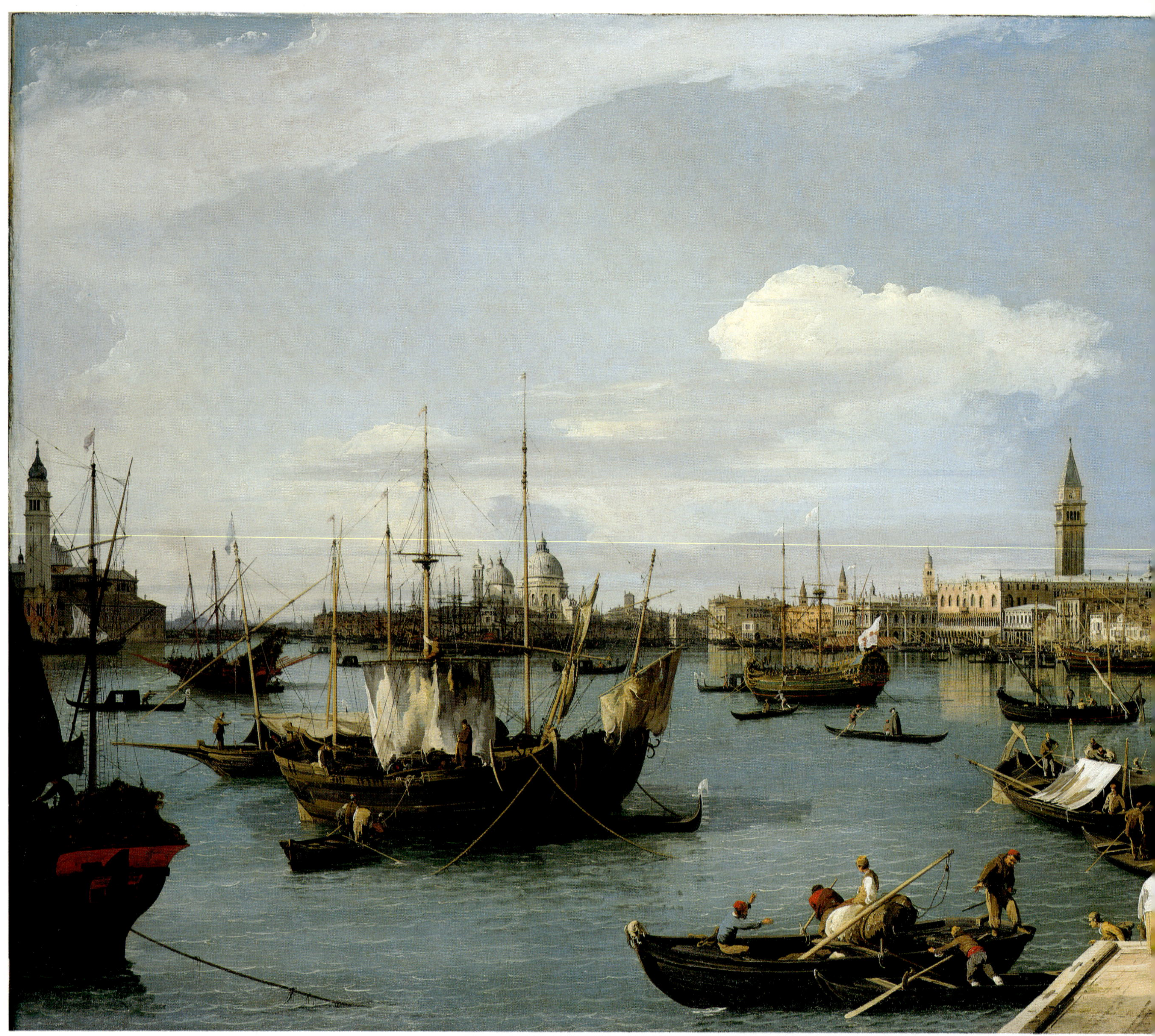

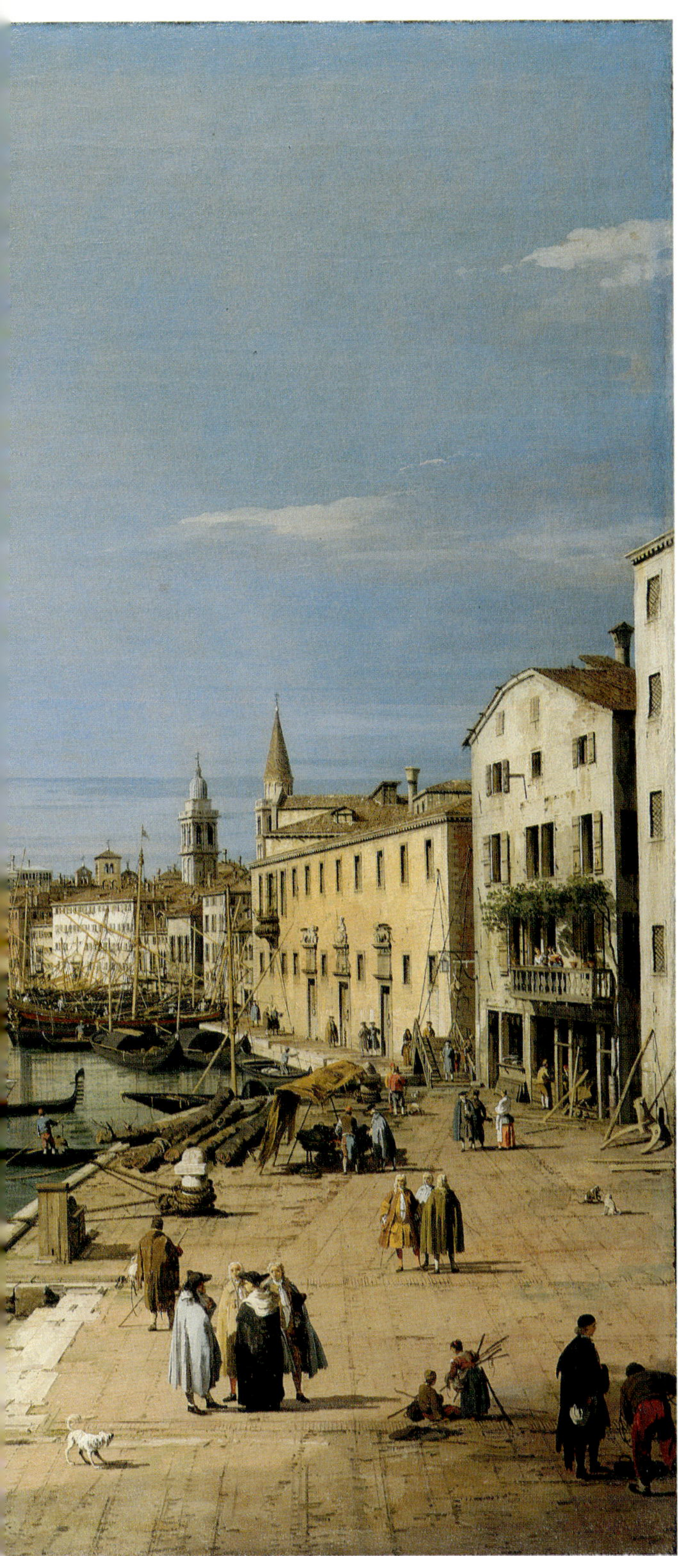

PL.1 Canaletto, *The Riva degli Schiavoni, looking West*, before 1736. Oil on canvas, 126.2 × 204.6 cm ($49\frac{11}{16} \times 80\frac{9}{16}$ in). London, Sir John Soane's Museum (no.P66).

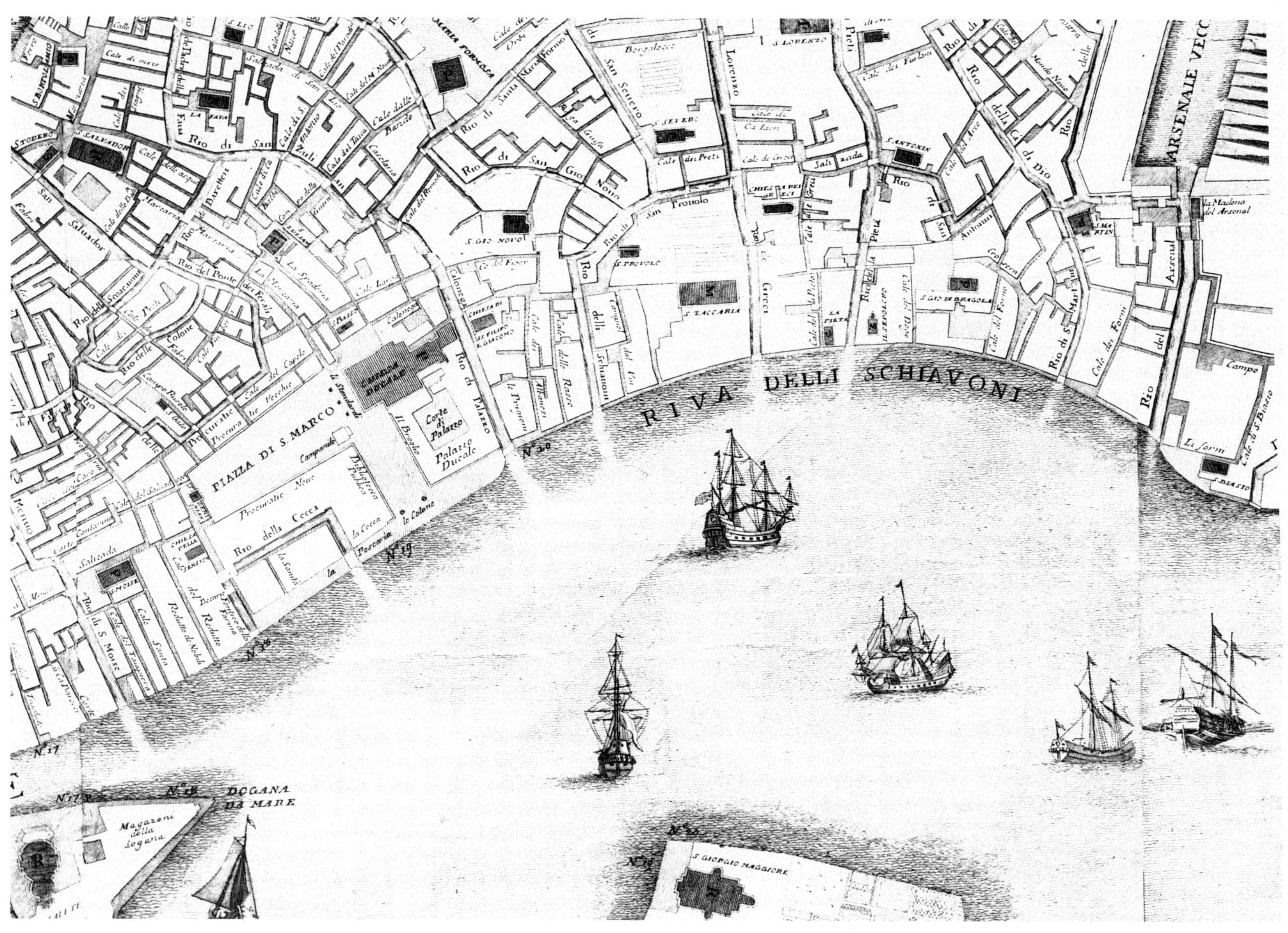
RIVA DELLI SCHIAVONI
PIAZZA DI S. MARCO
Palazzo Ducale
Corte di Palazzo
Procuratie Noue
Procuratie Vecchie
Campanile
Libreria Publica
Rio della Cecca
Rio di Palazzo
S. ZACCARIA
DOGANA DA MAR
Magazeni della dogana
S. GIORGIO MAGGIORE
ARSENALE VECCHIO
la Madona del Arsenal
S. LORENZO
S. ANTONIN
S. SEVERO
S. GIO NOVO
S. PROVOLO
S. GIO IN BRAGOLA
S. SALVADOR
Rio del Arsenal
S. BIASIO
Rio di S. Moise

Introduction

The Early Years

The first we hear of Giovanni Antonio Canal (1697–1768) is as an assistant to his father, Bernardo, an artist who, in 1719, was working in Rome as a painter of theatrical scenery. The family was Venetian, only one rung below patrician on the social ladder, and an artist did not lose status by becoming a scene painter; often his name would appear on the programme of an opera whereas the librettist's would not. The following year the son had given up the theatre and returned to Venice where he probably painted a number of capriccios in the manner of Sebastiano Ricci before setting up as a painter of Venetian views. He was then in his early twenties, and soon became known as Canaletto, the 'little Canal', to distinguish him from his father who had also returned to Venice. Nothing more is known of Bernardo, except a few signed views of mediocre quality, but he lived until 1744 and there is every likelihood that he in turn became his son's assistant. For Canaletto's success was immediate and before long it was being said that he delayed deliveries, charged too much, was difficult to deal with and even impertinent. This criticism need not be taken too seriously since it came mostly from middlemen who wanted to impress their clients with the value of their own services in dealing with an artist so much in demand.

The idea of using city streets as a subject for painting had originated in Holland in the 1650s and been taken to Rome by Gaspar van Wittel (known in Italy as Vanvitelli), who painted a few views of Venice when Canaletto was still a child. It was, though, Luca Carlevaris of Udine who founded the art in Venice with over a hundred engravings of the city's splendid buildings and a series of paintings, for the most part of the area near the Piazza S. Marco. Carlevaris must have had some success, although his interests were not confined to art, but when, in 1725, Stefano Conti, an early patron of Carlevaris, wanted more of his work he was advised by his agent that there was a new man whose pictures were astounding everyone who saw them and who, unlike Carlevaris, was able to make the sun shine in them. This was Canaletto.

It is true that Carlevaris's paintings fail to evoke the shimmer and luminosity of the Venetian light by which every visitor is captivated and he seems to have regarded his buildings as a background to a huge variety of figures rather than as his subject. However, the reference to Canaletto's sun is a little puzzling because the dazzling light we associate with his work was at that time still to come. The large, loosely-painted canvases known to have been produced before 1725 leave an impression of sombreness and drama rather than of sunshine. There are dark shadows in the foreground and the paint lies thickly on the coarse canvas which has been covered by a red ground.

FIG.1 The Riva degli Schiavoni from 'S. Biasio' [*sic*] and 'Le forni' (on the right, east) to the 'Palazzo Ducale' and 'La Cecca', the mint (on the left, west), from Lodovico Ughi's plan of Venice first published in 1729.
Note the narrowness of the Riva between the Piazzetta and S. Biagio and its true curve, which was exaggerated by Canaletto.

The figures often give the impression of having been painted hurriedly, leaving their clothes with ragged ends. But from the earliest period minute attention was being paid to distinguishing between the various textures of building materials depicted. The brick might be crumbling or freshly stuccoed, the stone of varying type, ancient or modern. Different colours were brushed into each other on the canvas to emphasize the distinction. Timber window frames or doors were generally picked out in black outlines; for these Canaletto had no hesitation in using a ruler where it would help, or any other instrument. Added to the artist's acute observation and originality of vision, the result was a painting that would sit comfortably in the gallery of any connoisseur and one that recalled the Venice that only Venetians knew.

Facing page, detail of PL.1

For it was international connoisseurs and Venetians, not tourists, who were Canaletto's patrons at this time, hence the fact that none of these early pictures is to be found in England where the greater part of his life's work still remains.[1] This dual appeal relates to the fact that, for all his paintings' apparent verisimilitude, from the very beginning Canaletto subordinated all other considerations to the creation of a work of art. Canaletto would not hesitate, when painting a scene in the Piazza S. Marco, to show the Campanile in its entirety even though only its base could be seen by an observer from the purported viewpoint. Having shown what could be seen from one viewpoint he would move to another for the rest of his picture, sometimes to a third. He would rearrange the curves of the Grand Canal or the Riva degli Schiavoni, change the angles of buildings or imagine himself at a non-existent viewpoint (examples of all three of these practices can be seen in the paintings in Sir John Soane's Museum). He would bring the background closer or move it farther away than it was in reality and he would include in his angle of vision perhaps the thirty degrees or so of the normal eye, perhaps twice or three times as much. In the words of one distinguished critic, he 'knew exactly how to take a great city to pieces and make new sense of it. This he did in ways that (as Van Gogh was to say in another context) are "not 'true' in a literal sense but truer than true." '[2]

Despite all these, and innumerable other 'adjustments' to the Venetian scene, the first patron to see a future for himself and Canaletto, by selling his work to the English, wrote of the artist that 'His excellence lyes in painting things as they fall immediately under his eye.' By this he could only have meant that Canaletto's views were topographically accurate, if lacking in imagination. How was such a judgement possible?

To answer the question we must turn to G.P. Guarienti, a contemporary, writing after Canaletto's great days were over but while he still had twenty-five years to live. 'He paints with such accuracy and cunning,' wrote Guarienti, 'that the eye is deceived and believes it is reality it sees, not a painting.'[3]

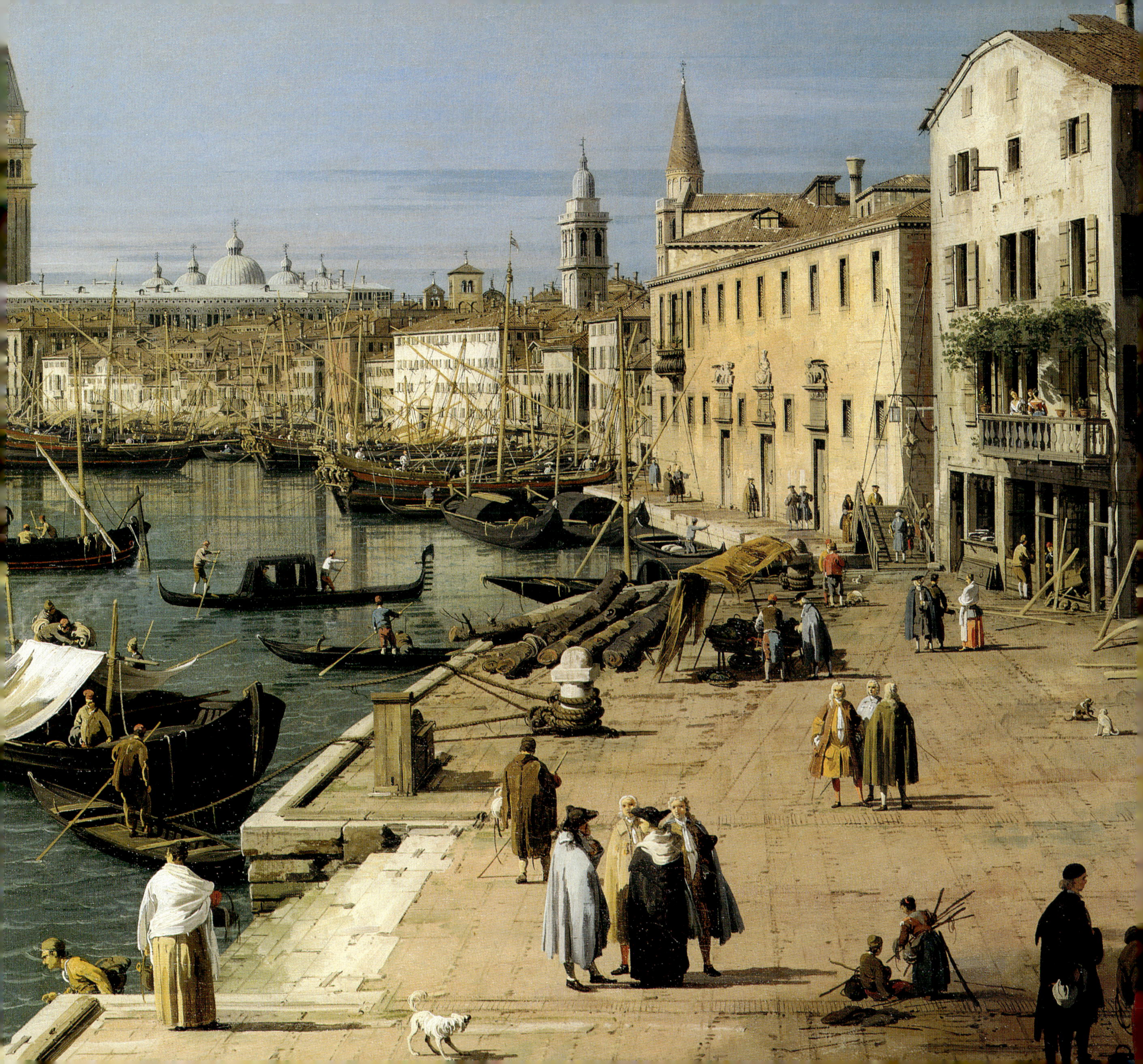

Two English Patrons

The writer of the words suggesting that Canaletto painted what fell immediately under his eye was Owen McSwiney, a failed Irish impresario from London, now living in Italy to escape his creditors, but supported by the Duke of Richmond for whom he bought and commissioned works of art – including two 'tomb paintings' in which Canaletto played a part. It is almost, if not quite, certain that it was McSwiney who first had the idea of diverting Canaletto from his large, theatrical paintings to small, sun-drenched mementoes of Venice as her English visitors might want to remember the city. From 1727 onwards he supplied the Duke of Richmond and others with a series of such views (in fact no more topographically accurate than any other of Canaletto's works), some of them painted on copper for the sake of the smooth surface (see FIG.4). McSwiney, though, was an ineffective charmer and before long his idea, and Canaletto himself, had been taken up by Joseph Smith, a highly successful businessman and collector, who spent his life in Venice and knew virtually everyone who passed through, above all the English.

The rest of the story is well known. Consul Smith, as he is generally known although he did not acquire the title until much later, became Canaletto's principal patron and agent and even McSwiney could get pictures out of the artist only by Smith's influence. Smith saw Canaletto through fifteen years of success and continued to befriend him when times became more difficult. Unlike McSwiney, Smith had few friends and posterity has not been kind to him. But he served Canaletto well while serving himself and, if he failed to be liked, he was at least respected.

There can be little doubt that the long association with Smith was of great benefit to Canaletto financially. Smith's contacts created an entirely new market for the artist's work and his studio prospered for more than ten years, also employing from 1735 onwards his nephew, Bernardo Bellotto, and no doubt one or two assistants at particularly busy times. Moreover, Smith knew the kind of picture he could sell and would have provided guidance on subject, size and, to some extent, manner. It is true that it was originally McSwiney, not Smith, who introduced Canaletto to the English and to the idea of painting small pictures for the walls of private houses rather than galleries, but McSwiney had few clients beyond the Duke of Richmond and lacked the business organization and reputation that Smith enjoyed. While it is not known how successful Canaletto was before the intervention of McSwiney and Smith, without them the market he was supplying must always have remained limited and there is no reason to suppose he could ever have expanded it on his own.[4] Finally, Smith was the ideal agent. He not only provided the pictures for his clients: he provided the frames, had them packed and shipped and, where necessary, found the finance – on all this, naturally, making a legitimate and not unreasonable profit for himself.

Smith's influence on Canaletto as an artist is more difficult to assess. It has often been suggested that under Smith Canaletto turned from poetry to prose, from an

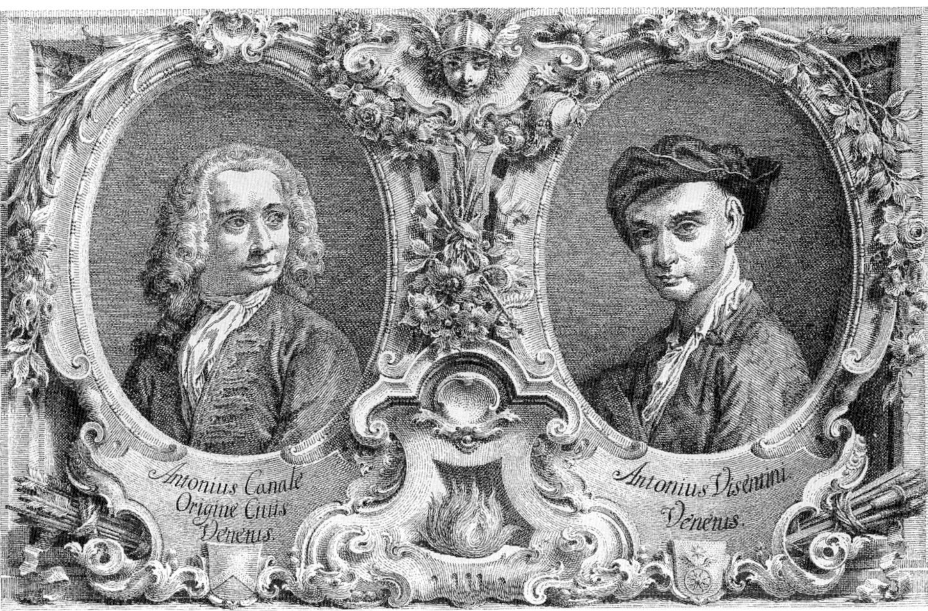

FIG.2 Canaletto and Visentini, as drawn and engraved by Antonio Visentini after a monochrome by G.B. Piazzetta for *Prospectus Magni Canalis Venetiarum*, Visentini's engravings after Canaletto's paintings first published in 1735. Canaletto, with wig and embroidered coat, is described by his rank whereas Visentini, simply dressed, is merely 'Venetian'.

Next page, detail of PL.1.

artist to a topographer. Such judgements can only be based on the vast number of copyists and followers generated by the success of Canaletto's studio. Little is known of the true facts – unanswerable questions arise at every turn when one examines Canaletto's career. There is good reason to suppose, though, that everything handled by Smith was of high, often of superb, quality. Those who dealt with Canaletto direct – for Smith had no monopoly of the studio's output – might find themselves with perfunctory or mechanical versions of the subjects they had chosen but the fastidious and knowledgeable might extract from Canaletto a supreme masterpiece such as *The Stonemason's Yard* (National Gallery, London), his earliest work to appear on public exhibition in England which went to an unknown buyer, or the splendid *Riva degli Schiavoni* which ended in Sir John Soane's possession.

There is no better way of judging Smith's plans for Canaletto than by considering his earliest commissions. First there were to be six great paintings of the Piazza and Piazzetta, on a par in size with most of the other pictures of the 1720s (over 170 cm high or wide – four of them were in upright form). Then, perhaps even before the six were finished, there was to be a series of twelve pictures forming a tour of the Grand Canal, not much larger than the views McSwiney had had painted with the English visitor in mind (47 cm high). Several years later, when these were all finished, a magnificent pair of 'Festival' pictures was added to the Grand Canal group (see FIG.3): even these were smaller (76 cm high) than Canaletto had been used to painting in the 1720s. The six Piazza pictures were almost certainly for a room in Smith's house at Mogliano on the mainland. Nothing similar to them was ever painted and Smith kept

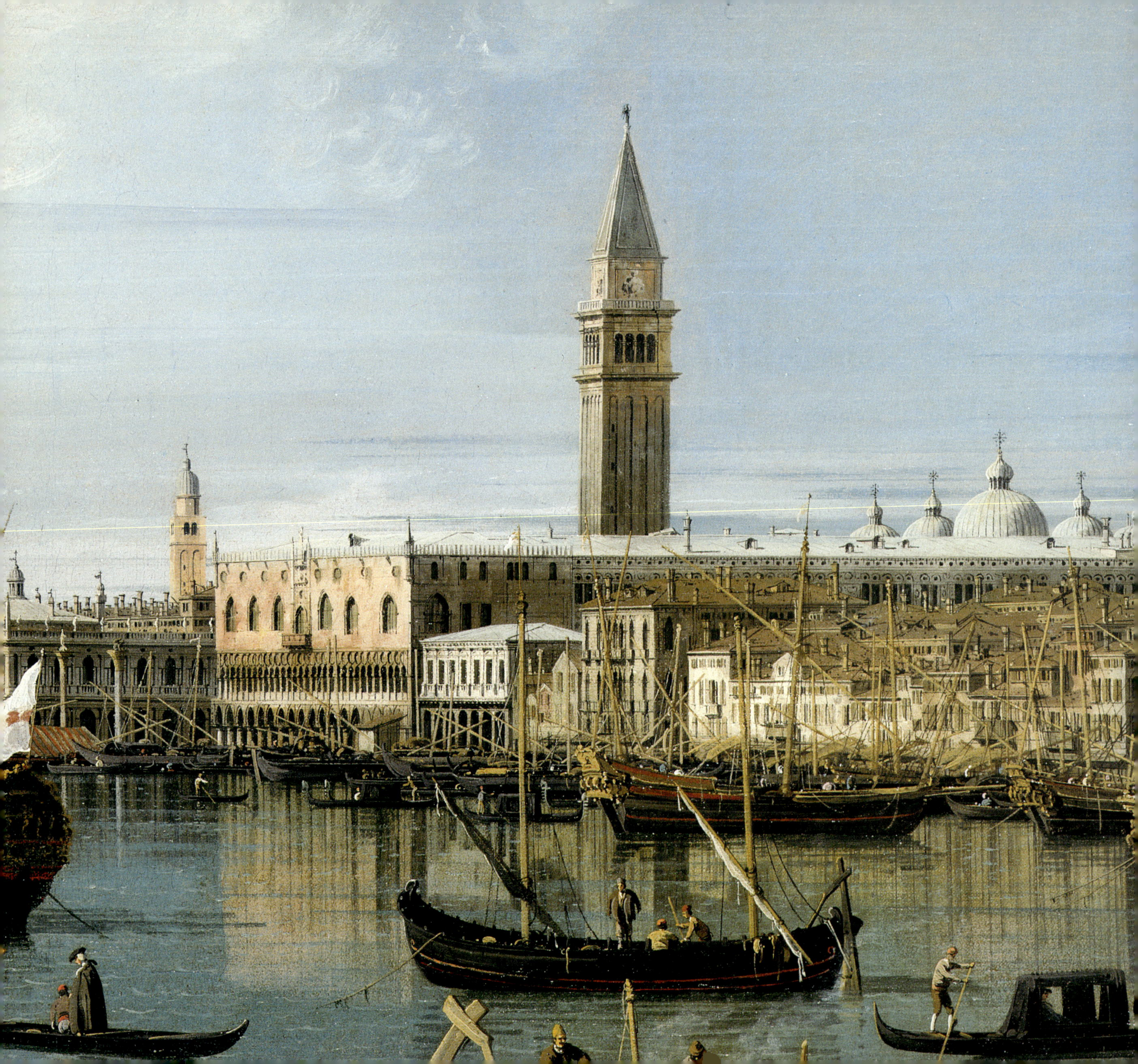

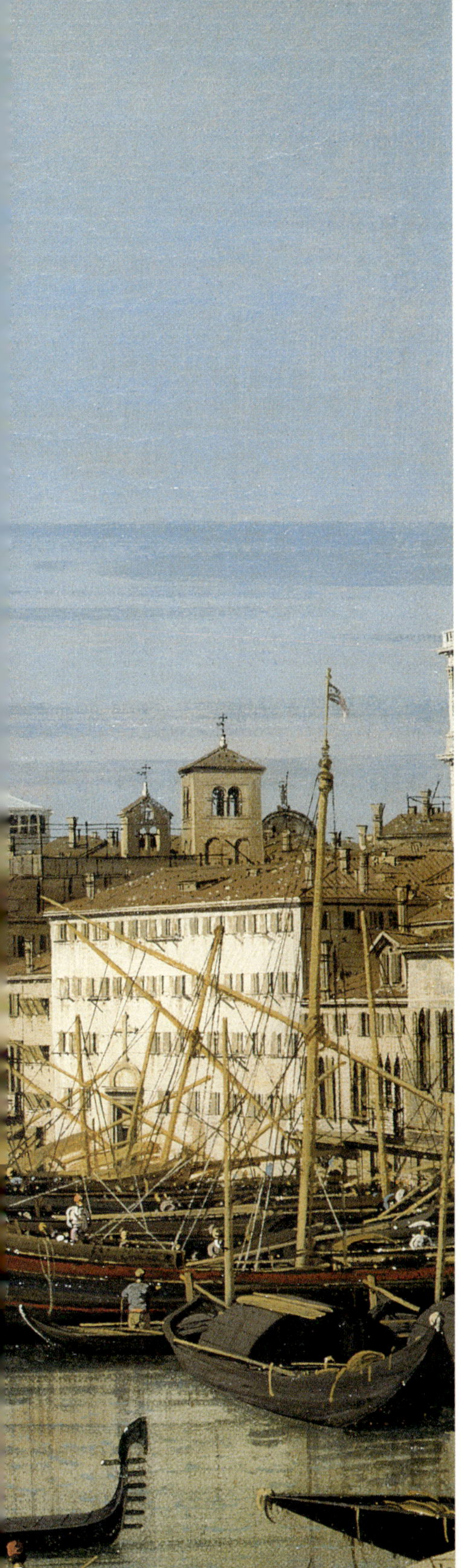

them until near the end of his life. Smith also kept the fourteen smaller pictures but their purpose was very different from the mere decoration of a room. They provided samples from which visitors were invited to place their orders, perhaps a specially painted version of the subject with the sky, figures and shipping changed, perhaps a subject of their own choice. The commissions might be for a single picture, a pair or even a group of two dozen or so (such as those now at Woburn Abbey).

In 1735 Smith's publishing house of Pasquali issued a set of engravings by Antonio Visentini of all fourteen paintings, together with the portraits of Canaletto and Visentini (FIG.2) and a title-page announcing that the originals were 'in the house of Joseph Smith, Englishman'. This referred to his house on the Grand Canal, just north of the Rialto Bridge, which can be seen in its original condition in one of the engravings. Characteristically, Smith had the painting itself altered to show the house as it was after he had it rebuilt by Visentini (who was also an architect). From these engravings collectors could place their orders without visiting Venice and those who could not hope to own a Canaletto painting could enjoy the engravings as a substitute. (Many will remember Mr Woodhouse, in Jane Austen's *Emma*, being comforted by 'some views of St Mark's Place, Venice', produced by Mr Knightley.)

The success of the enterprise may be judged by the number of surviving versions by Canaletto of the original Grand Canal pictures. There are, for instance, at least fifteen versions of *The Rialto Bridge from the North* apart from the one in Sir John Soane's collection (PL.2). The engravings also, of course, provided material for the many copyists and forgers whose work was supplied direct to visitors to Venice or, through agents, to undiscerning buyers in England or elsewhere.

A Change of Course

Well before 1735, when the engravings were published, Canaletto's new course had been set. In or about 1730 he changed his style to suit the smaller size of his paintings, the taste of his new kind of patron and, it must be admitted, the need to increase the output of his studio to meet the increased demand.

The red ground of his canvases was now changed to grey and, later, to a creamy beige. He no longer outlined the architectural details in black but developed a new technique demanding immense skill by which he loaded his brush with more than one colour and applied the light and dark paint in one stroke. The thick impasto of the 1720s was abandoned but the capital of a column would still sometimes be portrayed with a twist of a thickly-loaded brush. Later in the 1730s he would apply a thin layer of paint like a wash to increase translucency (just as, in his drawings, he began to use wash instead of his former hatching).

Canaletto's palette was always limited, a surprising fact in the light of the endless variety of tone in his architectural detail. The importance he attached to this is clearly shown by the notes he made in his sketchbooks using words such as *cene* (for *cenerino*, ash-coloured) and *Roseta sporco* (dirty reddish) to denote colour or, to indicate material, *Tole vecchie* (old weather-boarding) or *Tole* (tiles). He seems to have been fascinated by shops and stalls and the merchandise sold in them can often be clearly seen in his paintings. To ensure accuracy he therefore added to the sketches such notes as *Qual del lojo* (oil-shop), *Spicier* (grocer), *Stramacer* (mattress maker) or *Spechi* (mirrors). The rigging of the various craft he depicted carries total conviction to most laymen, although some maritime experts question it. The portrayal of sail-cloth, whether on vessels or land, aloft or furled, gave Canaletto the opportunity for some of his most dazzling displays of virtuosity.

In the large Piazza paintings of the 1720s the foreground figures are closely-studied portraits but at first the figures played a small part in the Grand Canal group. As the series grew they became larger and more carefully observed. By the time the two 'Festival' paintings were reached, about 1734, Canaletto had attained complete mastery of the handling of figures in all parts of the scene (see FIG.3). Those in PL.1 speak for themselves.

FIG.3 Canaletto, *The Bucintoro at the Molo on Ascension Day*, c. 1734–5. Oil on canvas, 77 × 126 cm (30¼ × 49½ in). H.M. the Queen, Windsor Castle, (no.ML397. WC314).

The Years of Prosperity

There is documentary evidence that Smith was selling Canaletto's paintings to the English in 1730 and, although the records reveal surprisingly little, no doubt whatever that he continued to do so for the following ten years. McSwiney, piqued by Smith's success in a field he had himself originated and by the preference Canaletto was obviously giving to Smith's requirements, had faded from the picture.

It was sometimes said at the time that Smith had a monopoly in Canaletto's output but this was untrue. Neither does he seem to have wanted one. All the paintings known to have passed through his hands are similar in size, except for the pair which sometimes rounded off a group, such as his own two 'Festival' pictures (see FIG.3) or the pair at Woburn Abbey. Nor did they vary very much in quality, which was uniformly high but seldom outstanding (again excepting those pairs). Canaletto was free to paint what he himself or other patrons wanted and the result was in some cases a picture painted on an off day, or with much studio assistance, in others a large masterpiece such as *The Stonemason's Yard*, *The Scuola S. Rocco* and *S. Simeone Piccolo* (all at the National Gallery, London), none of whose original owners is known, and Sir John Soane's *Riva degli Schiavoni*. Smith would have scorned the first category. He may well have preferred, too, to let others handle the occasional masterpieces on the grounds that it was safer to treat all his customers alike. He was a very experienced businessman – and he already had his own masterpieces in the form of the six great Piazza paintings.

Smith did not have to rely on the fourteen paintings engraved by Visentini for his stock. He acquired at least another twenty-four pictures of similar size which included views of *campi* (squares) as well as images of the Grand Canal. That Canaletto had lost

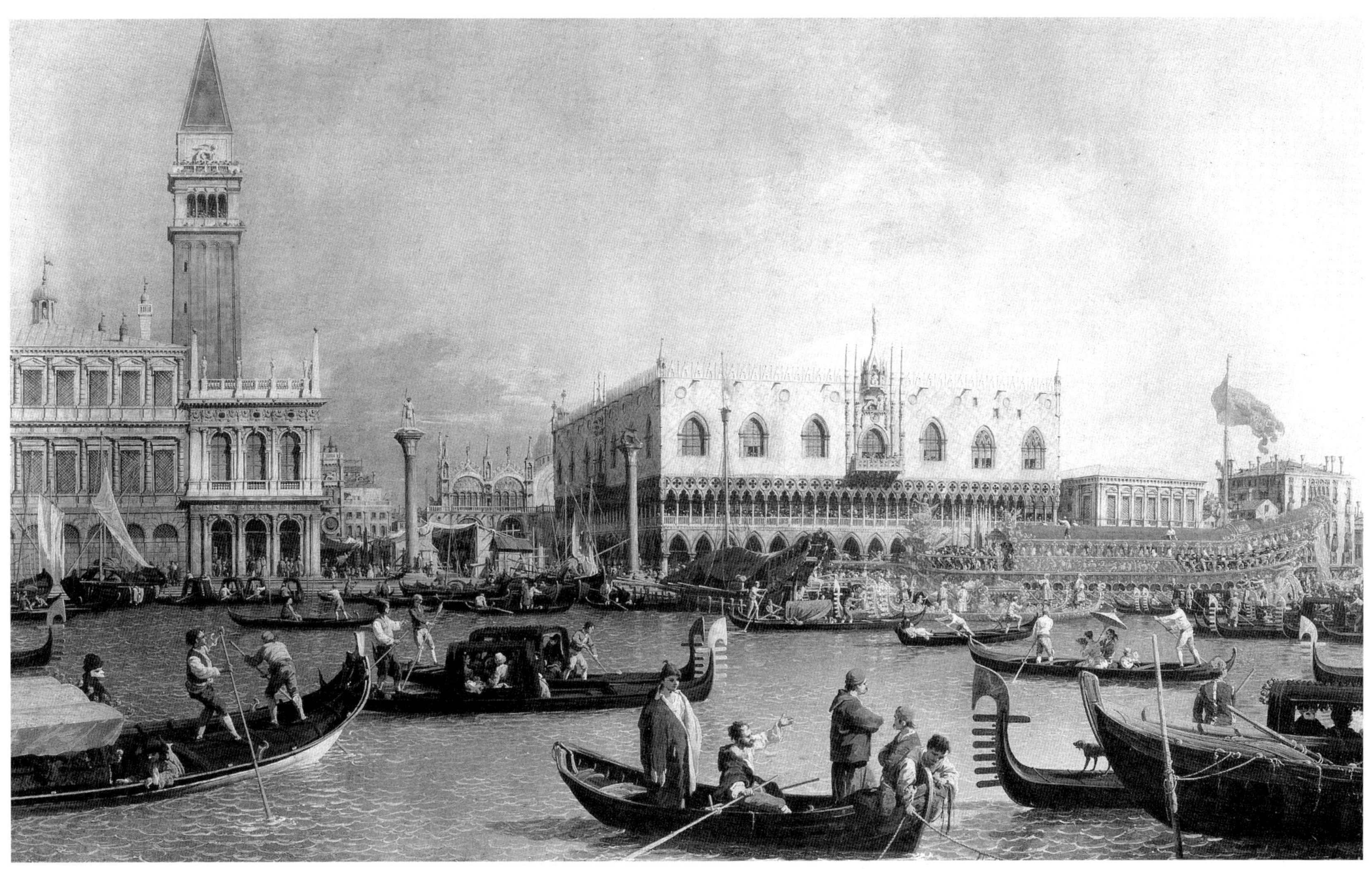

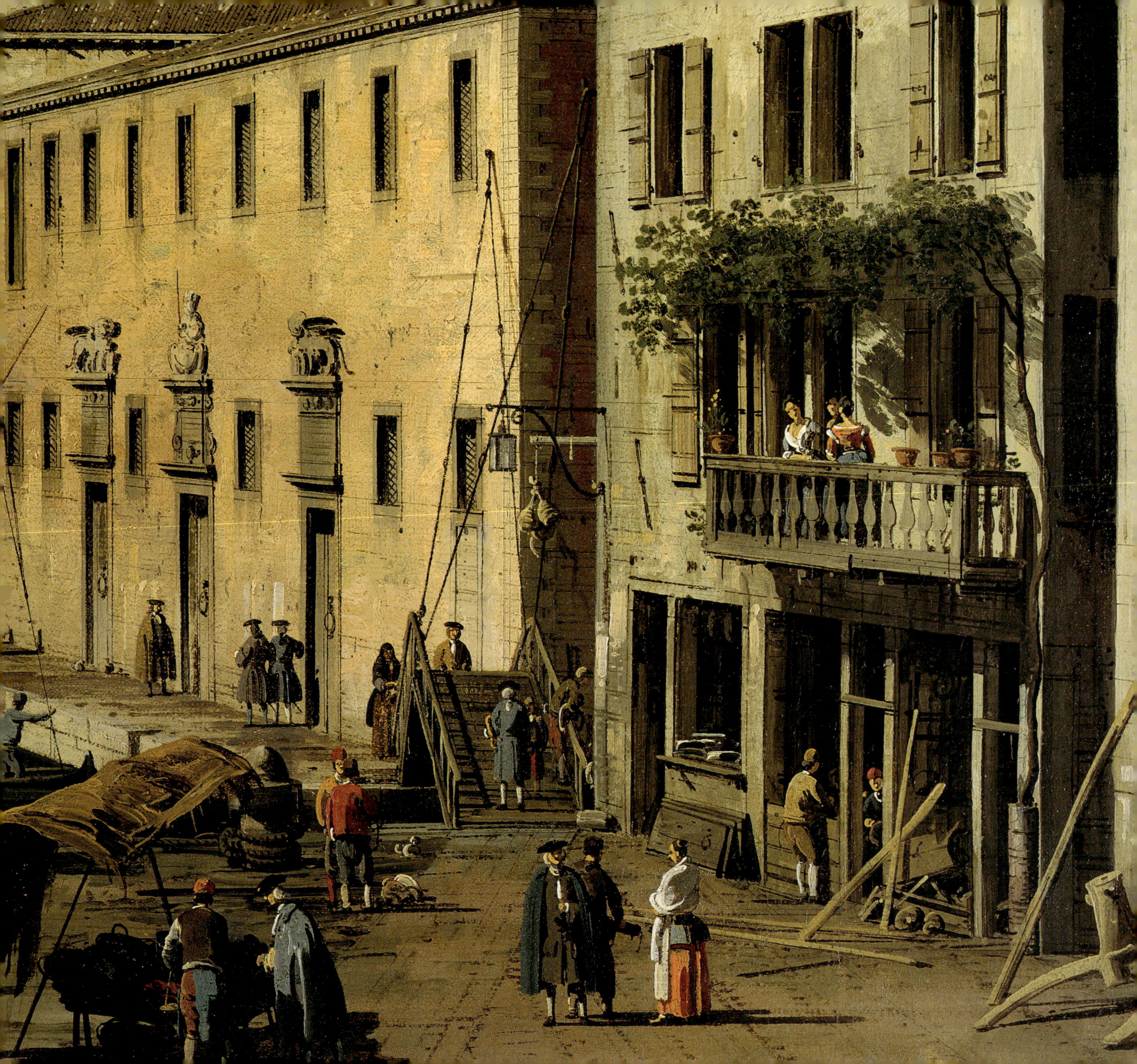

Facing page, detail of PL.1.

none of his cunning is evident particularly from the *campi* in which, by brilliantly skilful lighting and shadows, the viewer is made to feel that he knows what lies around a corner although he cannot see it and that behind the windows of the houses are people although they cannot be seen. Unlike the first fourteen paintings Smith was evidently willing to sell these pictures as well as take orders on them, and by the time they came to be engraved in 1742, he had only one left in his house.

The peak of the studio's prosperity came in about 1735 and it was at this time that Canaletto's nephew, Bernardo Bellotto, joined the other assistants, whose presence now became increasingly apparent in the studio's output. (Though there were never many assistants, as in the case of some other successful artists: two or three might even be an over-estimate.) Bellotto was then fifteen and, as would be expected, he played an expanding part in the studio production. There is no reason to suppose that he ever composed a picture himself while in Venice or that he was capable of achieving the subtleties of Canaletto's compositions. But he gradually developed a style of his own, lacking Canaletto's delicacy of touch while faithfully following his methods. By the time he left the studio in the early 1740s he was a fully-fledged artist of great skill and soon proved that he was able to compose in his own style. A number of versions of Canaletto subjects are recognised today as being wholly in Bellotto's hand; between these and Canaletto's wholly autograph work lie many paintings with passages which can only be attributed to Bellotto or other assistants of varying skill.

From Brush to Pen

The years in which Bellotto was working in the studio saw a change in Canaletto's style almost as great as between the 1720s and early 1730s, but now brought about by the need to save time rather than by the new patrons' taste. The artist no longer lingered over the difference between two adjoining columns. The figures still had plenty of movement but it was often the movement of mechanical dolls, the effect achieved by a flick of paint here, a twirl there and a couple of strokes to represent the body. In Canaletto's hands the brush was still capable of achieving striking effects but too often the method proved beyond the ability of assistants, even Bellotto.

At last, in the early 1740s, the pressure for more production eased and before long it had ceased altogether. The War of the Austrian Succession had reduced the number of visitors to Venice drastically and many English patrons had as many Canalettos on their walls as they wanted. Moreover, the first serious competitor to Canaletto had appeared in Michele Marieschi, who published a book of engraved views of Venice and was clearly prepared to supply original paintings if called upon. (He died the following year so the seriousness of the threat was never tested.)

Such were the considerations which must have led to the publication in 1742 of another twenty-four engravings based on the paintings which had passed through Smith's hands. This was by no means the only step taken by Smith and Canaletto to counteract the decline in demand for straightforward view painting. Canaletto had, from the beginning of his career, been as much at home with pen and paper as with brush and canvas. His drawings were of various kinds according to their purpose.

There was the preparatory sketch *in situ* for his own use in the studio when work on the canvas was to begin. Then there was the more detailed drawing, apparently intended to show a client what was proposed, subject to discussion and amendment. Finally, there was the finished drawing, occasionally commissioned by a publisher for engraving, more generally intended as a work of art in itself; some 150 of these have survived, the great majority once owned by Smith. Many of the latter were the subjects of paintings which had passed through Smith's hands, although by no means mere copies of the paintings such as Visentini had published. One group of drawings of the outskirts of Venice, quite unrelated to anything Canaletto had attempted before, is particularly brilliant in its power to evoke atmosphere and sunlight on paper, the pen being aided by a judicious use of wash. All Smith's drawings were kept by him and are now in the Royal Collection.

The same power to depict the fall of light without the use of colour is evident in a series of etchings dedicated to Smith as His Britannic Majesty's Consul, although certainly begun well before 1744 when that long-sought honour was at last conferred. The etchings varied in size and in type, *altre prese in Luoghi, altre ideate*, some done on the spot, others imagined. They display a subtlety and virtuosity which is quite extraordinary in an artist who, as far as is known, had never worked in the medium until his forties.

A number of the etchings reflect a tour of the Brenta and mainland which Canaletto undertook with Bellotto, no doubt instigated by Smith in a further effort to broaden his outlook. The journey also produced some fine drawings and, probably after the return to Venice, a few paintings.

Then there was a group of paintings of Rome, several of them bearing a signature and the date 1741 or 1742. Canaletto's reason for signing and dating paintings at this late stage is obscure and there is no reason to suppose that he ever returned to Rome after leaving it in his early twenties. Bellotto certainly went there and the likelihood is that, on his return, Canaletto used his nephew's and his own early drawings as the basis for yet another departure in his work.

Canaletto in England

It was to no avail. By 1746 it must have been evident that Venice had no more to offer Canaletto, and Smith, always the loyal friend, urged him to turn to England where so many of his admirers would surely welcome him. McSwiney had himself returned some years earlier and Smith wrote with a request that he should introduce Canaletto to his old patron, the Duke of Richmond. This led, although not for some time, to the two marvellous views still at Goodwood House and Canaletto somehow managed to get taken up by Sir Hugh Smithson, later Duke of Northumberland, who became his best

FIG.4 Canaletto, *The Rialto Bridge from the North*, 1727. Oil on copper, 46 × 58.5 cm (18 × 23 in). The Duke of Richmond and Gordon, Goodwood (no.232).

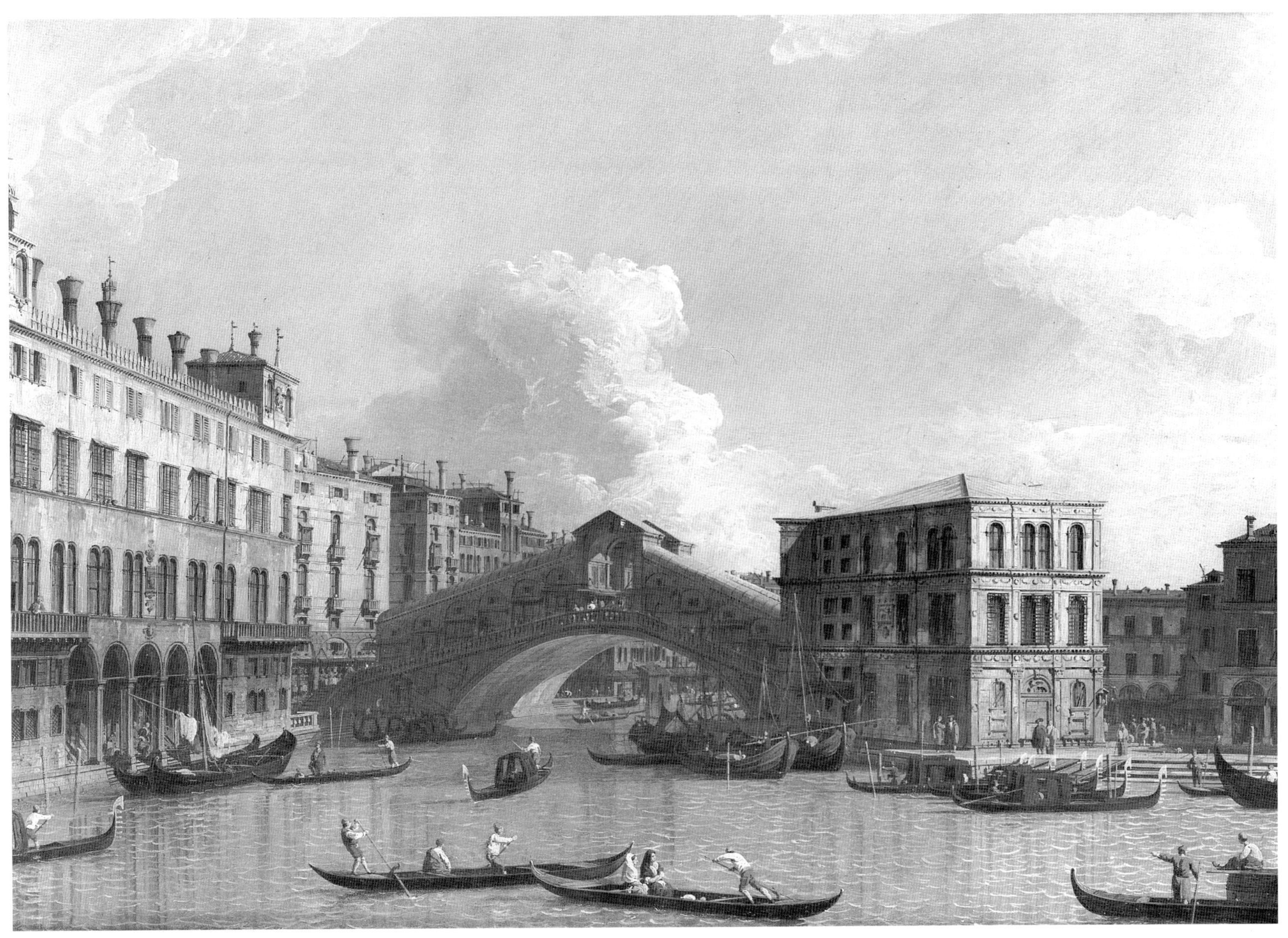

patron and brought in other Commissioners of Westminster Bridge, which had just been completed and which provided material for many of the early paintings and drawings. The Commissioners included the Duke of Beaufort, for whom Canaletto painted a view of Badminton Park. Sir Hugh also introduced the artist to Lord Brooke, later Earl of Warwick, for whom he produced the celebrated views of Warwick Castle.

Again the time came when everyone who wanted, and could afford, Canalettos had as many as he needed. The artist returned to Venice where conditions, it seemed, were no better and so went back to London where two or three new patrons were found.

Facing page, detail of PL.1.

The Final Years

After some nine years in England Canaletto finally returned permanently to Venice. He was almost sixty, with a dozen more years to live, and Smith was in his eighties (he had only recently married 'a beauteous virgin of forty', as Lady Mary Wortley Montagu described her). Smith even added a little to his collection of over fifty paintings and 150 drawings by Canaletto before selling almost all his pictures, books and cameos to George III in 1762. The Canalettos have remained in the Royal Collection ever since.

It is hard to know how Canaletto filled his time during those years, for most of which his imagination seems to have deserted him. He painted subjects he had already drawn or etched, worked for engravers, and was once seen drawing in the Piazza by an Englishman on his Grand Tour with his bear-leader. They recognised the artist, were given his drawing and taken to his studio where he was persuaded to allow them to buy a large painting of London which he had not previously been able to find it in his heart to part with. It is hard to resist the conclusion that these events followed a sequence carefully planned by Canaletto.

There were times when the Canaletto whose 'work was astounding everyone in Venice' (as Stefano Conti had been told) reappeared. In 1763 he was at last elected to the Academy of Fine Arts and painted a large panorama of the Piazza which in a way summed up his life's work (FIG.23). A German merchant, Sigismund Streit, returning home after a lifetime in Venice, took with him four views including two which would have done credit to Canaletto in his greatest days of fame and achievement. His last drawing was, as he wrote below it, of the musicians who sing in the Ducal Church of S. Marco, 'done by me at the age of 68, without spectacles, in the year 1766'. He died on 19 April 1768 and had twelve priests and candles at his funeral, as befitted his rank, but he left very little to his sisters, the only family he ever had.

'In painting views of Venice', wrote a French connoisseur at the height of Canaletto's fame, 'he far surpasses any other artist ever ... but one can no longer afford to buy anything from him.'[5]

'There are no more view painters of repute', the sculptor, Antonio Canova, was told in 1804 when he hoped to buy the work of someone inspired by Canaletto. 'What a pity it is.'[6]

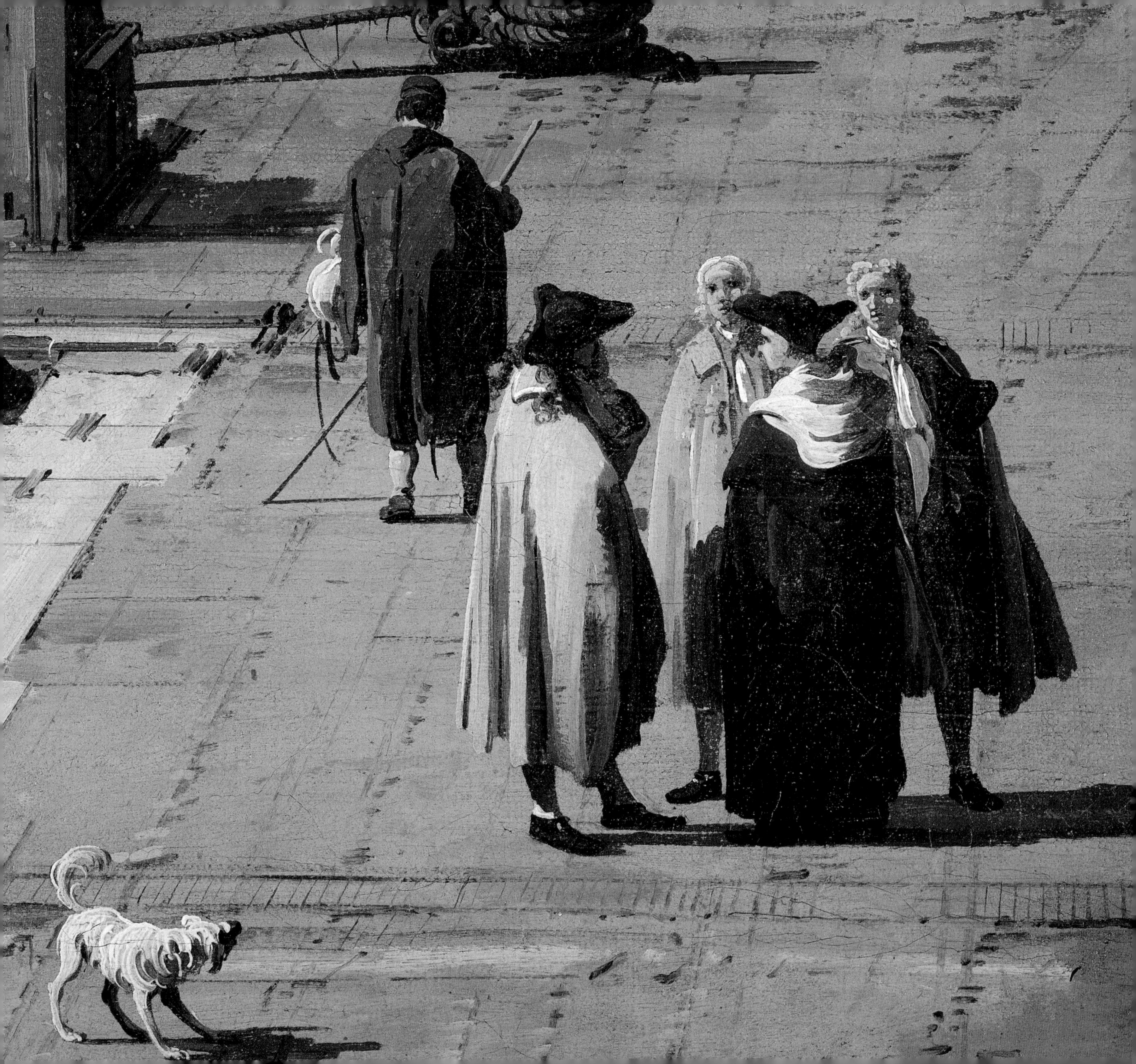

The Pictures

The Riva degli Schiavoni, looking West

Oil on canvas, 126.2 × 204.6cm (49 11/16 × 80 9/16 in), before 1736

Many of today's visitors must leave Venice without having seen this wonderful view. This would have amazed the Venetians for it is from here that the Arsenal is reached. For the first 400 years of Venetian tourism the Arsenal was one of the first sights distinguished visitors were taken to. When Dante described his visit in 1321 the Arsenal was at least 200 years old although until then its secrets had been known to few. Today it is desolate and offers nothing to the visitor except a short cut for the *circolare* water bus, a museum of naval history and an entrance which is the earliest renaissance building in Venice. Others who pass Canaletto's viewpoint might be on their way to the *Biennale* exhibition but, with so much else to see, not many find time for a walk as far as this along the Riva just for pleasure. It can hardly have been a popular view even by Canaletto's time for he painted the scene but twice (and it perhaps played a part in some other versions) whereas there are more than a dozen authentic examples of the view in the opposite direction from viewpoints close to the Doge's Palace (FIG.5).

There was no broad highway leading to the Arsenal as there is now (FIG.6). The view is from a window in the church of S. Biagio which was built on a tongue of land which provides the foreground of the picture and was the first point at which Venetians could congregate between here and the Doge's Palace. Until the 1780s the Riva was no wider than its bridges as can be seen from FIG.1.

A smaller version of the picture, now in Vienna, taken from a lower viewpoint farther to the left, is worth considering at this point if only to compare the house with the balcony in the right foreground (FIG.10). In the Vienna version the balcony is of wood with makeshift timber brackets and one might hesitate to sit on it. In the Soane picture this has been replaced by a stone balcony and the house has been generally renovated. The mature vine over the balcony seems to have been lost in course of the work and to have been replaced by younger plants. Canaletto might exaggerate the curve of the Riva and include a wider view than the eye could encompass, as he has in both versions, but in matters such as a new balcony his accuracy could be trusted.

The balconied house has gone but the buildings beyond it, which also seem to have enjoyed refurbishment between the two versions, were the Forni, the military bakeries, and are still standing. Between the house and the Forni stands a bridge, apparently modest but in fact crossing one of the most important *rii*, or small canals, in Venice,

FIG.5 Canaletto, *The Riva degli Schiavoni, looking East*, early 1740s. Oil on canvas, 58.2 × 93.5cm (23 × 36 1/2 in). London, The Wallace Collection (no.P509). This is one of many examples of this scene by Canaletto and his followers, generally, as here, purporting to be from a high viewpoint over the water. In this case, unusually, both the columns of Saint Theodore and Saint Mark are shown on the left, followed by the Doge's Palace and the Prison. The first large building on the Riva beyond the Palace is now the Danieli hotel, the second the Church of the Pietà, beyond which is the steeple of the campanile of S. Giovanni in Bragora, which is seen on the right of the Soane *Riva* (PL.1) and in drawings from a similar viewpoint. By the time this work was painted, in the early 1740s, Canaletto's work had become rather mechanical, as can be seen by comparison with PL.1.

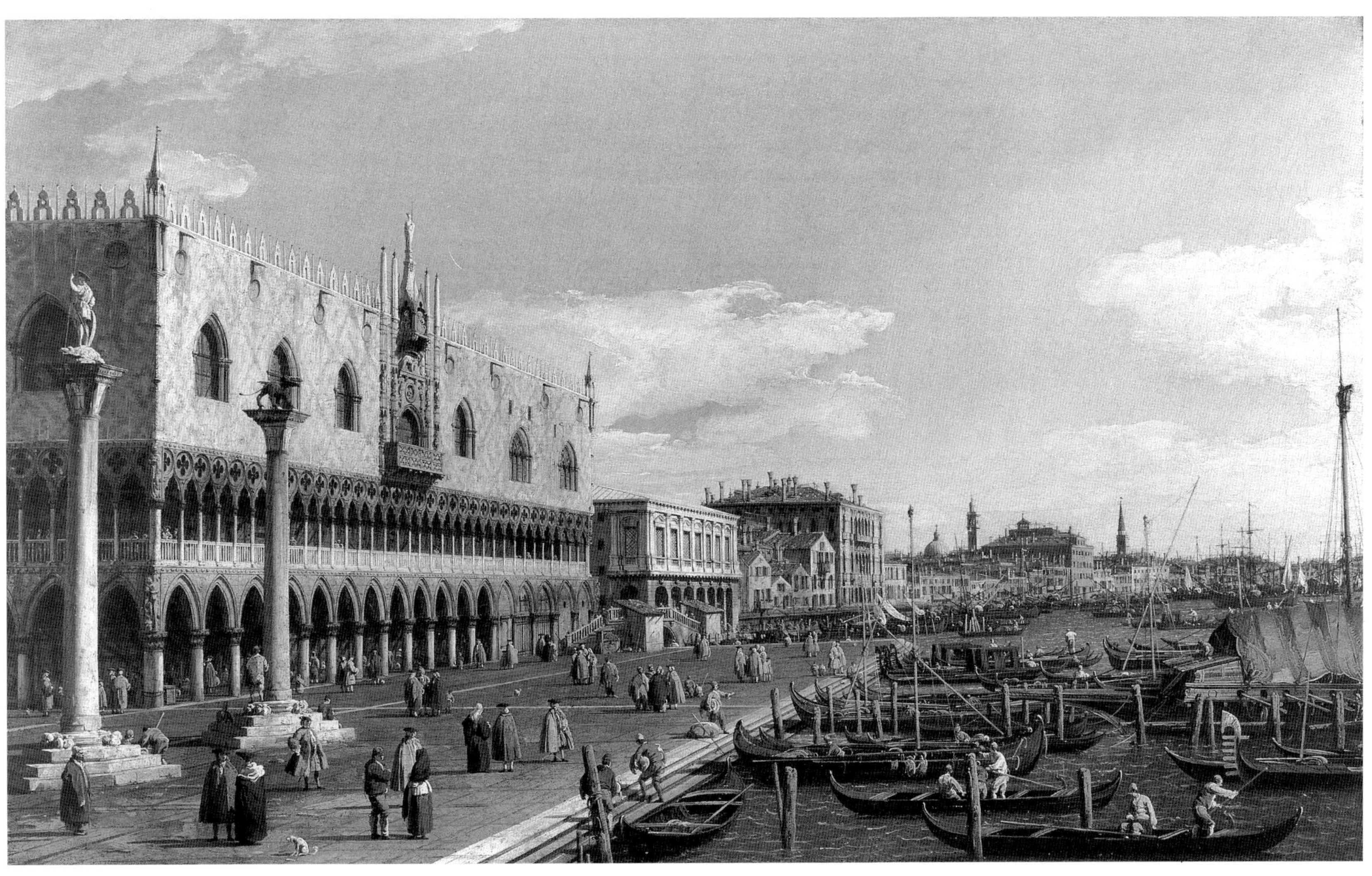

which provided the only access from the Bacino to the Arsenal (see FIG.1).

Jacopo de' Barbari's plan of Venice of 1500 shows this bridge as a single-span platform which could be raised by ropes. The bridge shown in Canaletto's painting was built towards the end of the 17th century and is often assumed to have been a drawbridge. Such is the detail with which he has painted it, however, that it is clear that the cables are firmly fixed to the walls of the Forni and the balconied house and could not be drawn up. Nor is there the hinge mounting on the Riva which would be expected in a drawbridge. There can be little doubt that when it was necessary for a vessel to pass along the canal the two sections of the bridge were manhandled apart along the quay, the central parts still swinging on the cables.

Canaletto's bridge was replaced in 1788 when it is recorded that the Forni were being seriously damaged by 'the heavy chain fixed on the external corner of the building which took the weight of half of the movable wooden bridge'. A swivelling bridge was substituted which lasted until 1824, when it was replaced by another of similar design which served until the 1930s; the present stone bridge was then built over a much-widened canal.[7]

Beyond the Forni the eye is led past a string of undistinguished buildings to the Prison and the Doge's Palace, above which soars the Campanile, then across the entrance to the Grand Canal (with a glimpse up the canal), to the Salute and so across the Giudecca Canal to the island of S. Giorgio Maggiore, which would certainly be invisible unless the viewer were to turn his head. The foreground, so full of detail, and this huge sweep of buildings in the background are held together by a superb study of the Bacino (the basin or harbour) of S. Marco with every variety of craft from barges, sandolos and gondolas to a schooner flying the English flag. It is hard to resist a feeling that the painting is the forerunner of, and perhaps the inspiration for, another masterpiece by Canaletto, a view of the *Bacino di S. Marco* looking in the opposite direction (FIG.11) in which, incidentally, Canaletto combines different viewpoints to great effect.

By the time he came to paint the Soane *Riva* Canaletto must have known the scene well. He had painted the version now in Vienna (FIG.10) and he had made three drawings. The first, which was taken away by Bellotto when he left the studio, is a free sketch which might have been made from a low window of S. Biagio or even from the ground in front of the church (FIG.8). From this he made a rather more finished drawing (FIG.9) which he gave or sold to Smith. Surprisingly, Smith also owned another drawing, not illustrated here, more finished still and from the same viewpoint but with entirely different figures and shipping. It looks as if the Vienna painting might have passed through Smith's hands with him keeping the two drawings as a sort of substitute – the collector and the businessman in Smith's character must often have been at loggerheads and there are many instances of his keeping drawings closely related to paintings known to have been sold by him. However, there is no other evidence to link Smith with the Vienna painting, which it has been suggested may have been bought by the

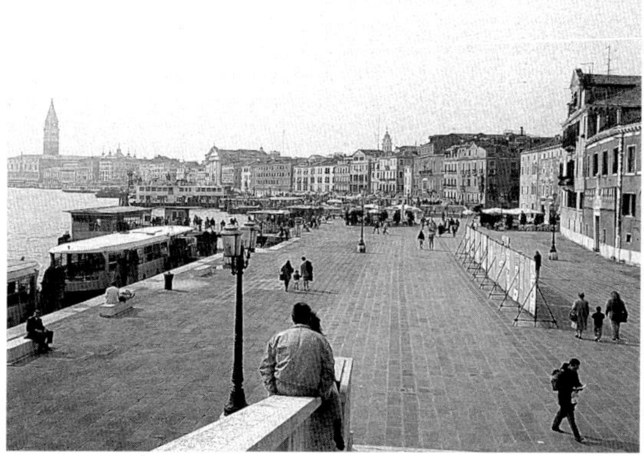

6

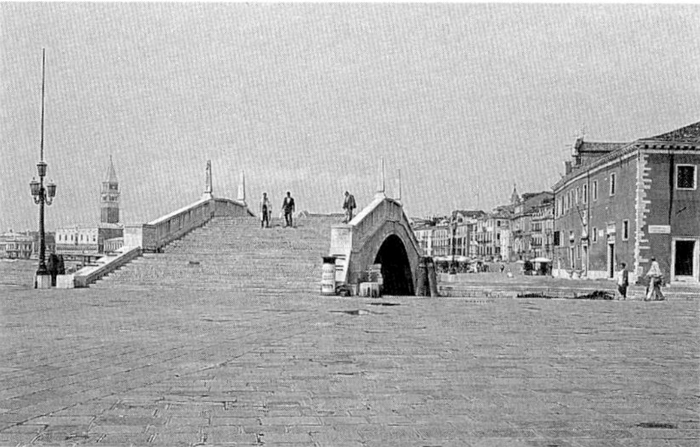

7

Facing page
FIG.6 The view from the modern Arsenal bridge, about 50 m east of Canaletto's viewpoint for the Soane *Riva*.

FIG.7 The modern Arsenal bridge, from about Canaletto's viewpoint for the Soane *Riva*.

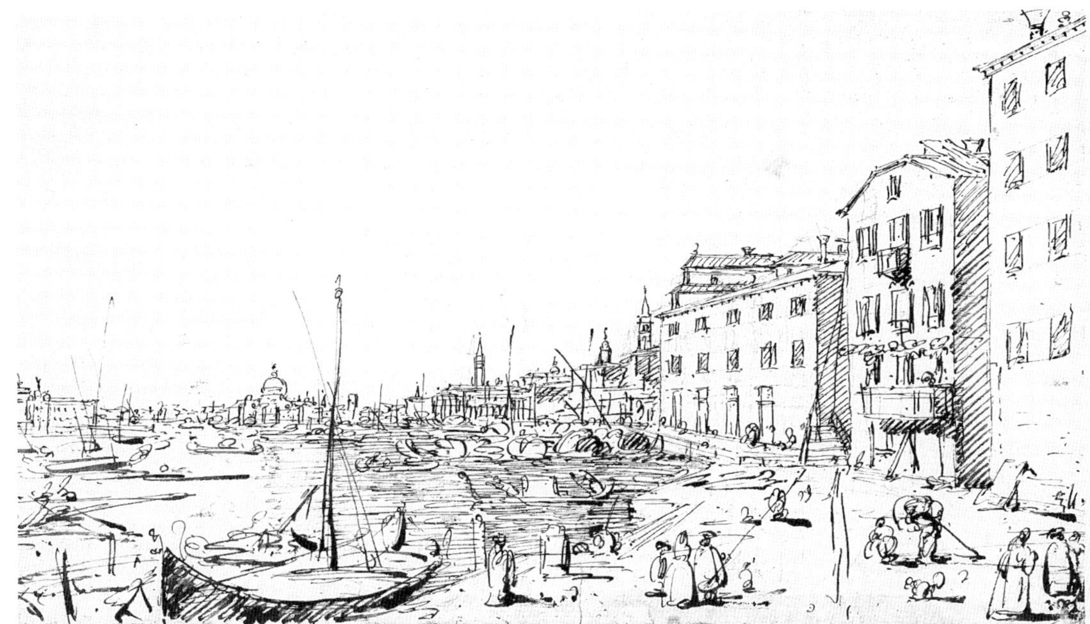

FIG.8 Canaletto, *The Riva degli Schiavoni, looking West*, after 1726–8. Pen and brown ink, 23 × 38.5 cm (9 × 15 1/8 in). Darmstadt, Kupferstichkabinett (no.A.E.2198).
The viewpoint is close, but not identical, to the painting now in Vienna (FIG.10), suggesting that another drawing must have been used for the painting itself. Bellotto took this drawing with him when he left Canaletto's studio and there are indications that he made additions to it in his own hand. Smith owned a drawing with figures and shipping much the same, but more finished (Royal Collection, RL7455), as well as the drawing shown in FIG.9.

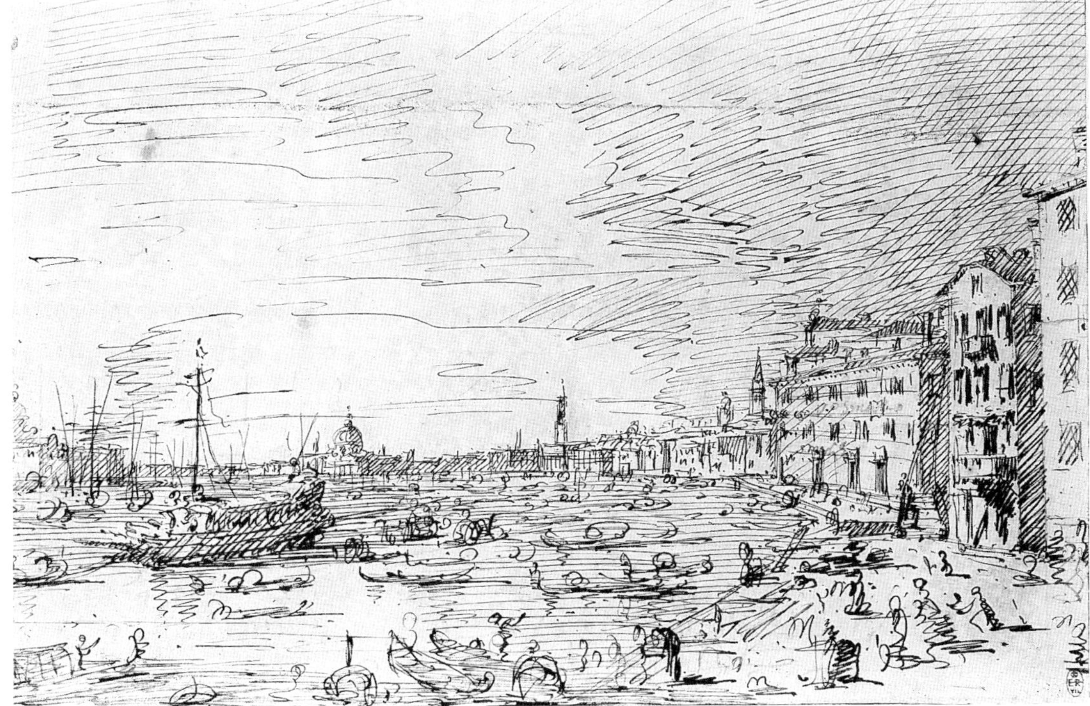

FIG.9 Canaletto, *The Riva degli Schiavoni, looking West*, c. 1729. Pen and brown ink over pencil, 21.2 × 31.7 cm (8 1/2 × 12 1/2 in). H.M. The Queen, Windsor Castle (no.RL7457).
As well as the more finished drawing based on FIG.8, Joseph Smith owned this drawing, which appears to be taken from almost the same viewpoint (compare the position of the two campaniles just beyond the Forni). It is certainly related to the Vienna painting (FIG.10) rather than to the Soane version, and Smith's ownership of the drawing suggests that the former painting may have passed through his hands. Apart from this suggestion, however, the drawing seems to have been made after the painting and FIG.8 rather than preceding them.

Prince of Liechtenstein, never a client of Smith's. Nothing is really known of its origin, not even whether it was ever seen by the buyer of the much more important Soane version, Marshal Schulenburg (see below).

For the Soane painting there must have been preparatory drawings, made from the higher viewpoint to the right of the one used for the drawings reproduced (FIGS 8 and 9). They would have shown the greater foreshortening of the Forni and the different positions of the two campanile, particularly that of the straight-sided steeple of S. Giovanni in Bragora, in the Soane picture seen above the Forni (the steeple is now demolished: that of S. Giorgio dei Greci survives, though leaning). No drawings have survived, though, so we shall never know how Canaletto drew that new balcony in the foreground which he painted so lovingly.

Is this a marine picture? Three quarters of it records the multifarious shipping that was to be seen every day in the Pool of Venice. Each vessel seems to be occupied by a crew about their daily duties. The water reflects the dazzling architecture as only seems possible in Venetian light.

Or is it an architectural painting, with the modest houses of the foreground lovingly portrayed in minute detail, leading away to some of the most celebrated buildings in the world? Or a 'genre' picture, painted to show the Venetians gathered in groups for their unceasing talk, the very texture of their clothes made evident by a few brushstrokes?

Few of us will place the *Riva degli Schiavoni* in any of these categories. By his precision of touch, the subtleties of his use of light and shade, by his skilful blending of the qualities of sky and water with every variety of timber, stone and other building materials, Canaletto has surely created a work of art of total harmony and order.

History

Sir John Soane's *Riva degli Schiavoni* is a rare, if not unique, example of a Canaletto painting whose history can be traced from its origin, although it was never handled by Joseph Smith. Its first owner was Marshal Johann Matthias Schulenburg, a professional soldier born in Saxony in 1661. In 1715 the Venetians turned to him to defend them against the Turkish attacks on Corfu and this he did brilliantly. For this he was granted a generous pension, a statue was erected to him in the courtyard of the Arsenal and he was given a Gothic palace on the Grand Canal near S. Trovaso (now known as Palazzo Loredan dell'Ambasciatore). He accordingly spent much of his time in Venice, advising the Republic on military matters. He began collecting paintings and sculpture in 1724 and built up a huge collection before his death at the age of 87. This was sent, over a period of time, to Germany where, like so many collectors, Schulenburg hoped it would remain in a permanent gallery as a memorial to himself; the hope was not fulfilled but vestiges of the collection still remain with his family.

Schulenburg's reputation is not that of a discerning collector and he was more interested in history painting and portraits than views. He nevertheless owned some

FIG.10 Canaletto, *The Riva degli Schiavoni, looking West*, before 1736. Oil on canvas, 42 × 62.5 cm (18 × 24½ in). Vienna, Gemäldegalerie, (no.GG6332).

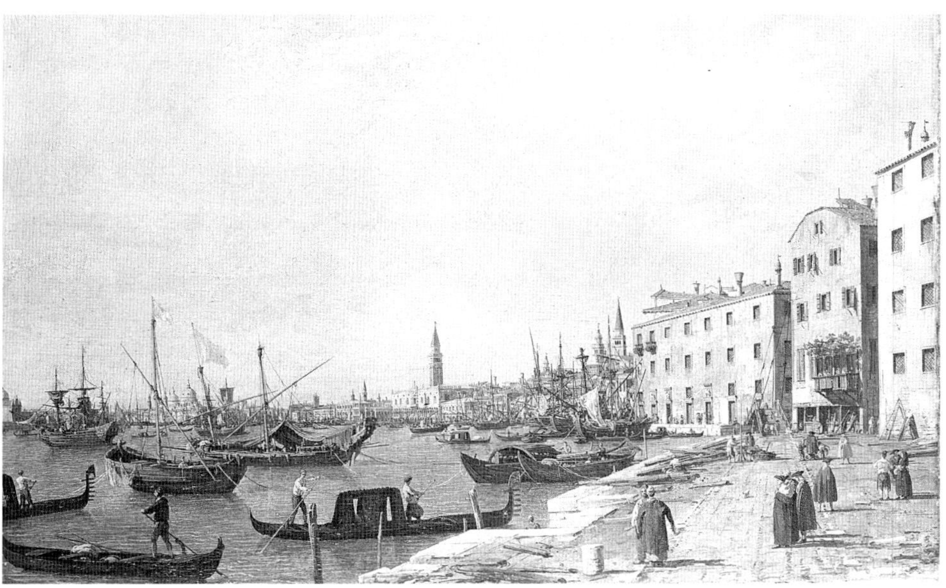

works by Carlevaris and, much later, by Marieschi and he commissioned a view of Corfu, the scene of his triumph, from Canaletto. In addition to the large *Riva* he bought two small paintings of the Piazza S. Marco from Canaletto and two capriccios, one of which has recently come to light.[8]

There is no evidence to connect Schulenburg's *Riva* with the version now in Vienna (FIG.10). He may have seen the latter, perhaps in Smith's house, and commissioned one of Canaletto's rare large paintings based on it. Alternatively, it may have been painted by Canaletto for his own pleasure and remained in the studio awaiting a buyer. One can only speculate.

Certainty comes with descriptions in Schulenburg's catalogues and accounts of a picture (*quadro*) described as 'leading from S. Biagio as far as the Salute' for which Canaletto was paid 100 *zecchini* (about £55) 'on account' of a bill for 120 *zecchini* on 23 February 1736. This must refer to the *Riva* painting which, in a catalogue of the collection dated 30 May 1738, was described as 'a view of the S. Biagio region towards the Salute and the Grand Canal with many very grand vessels, both of war and cargo, and many beautiful figures, buildings and boats'.[9] The price was high, as much as Conti had paid for all four of his views, but the picture was twice the size of Conti's and ten years had passed during which Canaletto's fame had burgeoned. In 1734–5, when the picture was probably painted, he was indeed at the height of his powers in the style he had adopted under Smith's influence; this was the period when he had painted the two great 'Festival' pictures which concluded the Grand Canal series (FIG.3). It was also the period when the pressure on the studio had almost reached its peak. In 1748, when demand had fallen to such an extent as to drive Canaletto from Venice to England and his reputation must have suffered accordingly, G.B. Piazzetta (who had painted the portraits reproduced in FIG.2) was called in to catalogue Schulenburg's collection. He valued the *Riva* at more than three times as much as it had cost, a high tribute to Canaletto from one who was said to be reluctant to recognise the talents of other artists.

Schulenburg had died the previous year but his collection was kept together for almost 30 years. In 1775, though, his family sold 125 of his paintings at Christie's in London including the *Riva* and the two small views of the Piazza S. Marco referred to above. These had been bought in 1731 for 62 *zecchini*, just under £30 the pair, a good price but, for their size, 25 by 37 inches, not much above what Smith is known to have been charging the English at the time. They were described in the catalogue as 'remarkably fine, the best time of the master' which would be true of pictures of that date. One was sold for 28 guineas and the other withdrawn at 21 guineas. The *Riva* was described as 'A capital view of Venice, the best known of the master'. Whatever that was intended to mean it failed to attract a buyer at the reserve and the picture was bought in at 199 guineas, almost four times as much as Canaletto had received in 1736 and even more than Piazzetta's valuation of 1748.

Some time after this the *Riva* must have been bought by Charles-Alexandre Calonne, at one time the Finance Minister of France and a prominent collector. After Calonne's dismissal by Louis XVI he lived in England and sold most of his collection. In 1795 he is recorded as having sold for 165 guineas at Skinner's auction rooms a picture by Canaletto of 'The Grand Canal', which can only have been his *Riva*.

The next owner was William Beckford (1759–1844) who at the age of eleven had inherited from his father a vast fortune, most of which he spent on indulging in his eccentricities, especially building at the family home at Fonthill Splendens, Wiltshire. His one literary achievement was the short oriental novel, *Vathek*, but his letters from Italy, Spain and Portugal are still often quoted in travel books. These were written while Beckford was travelling at the age of twenty but were not properly published until fifty years later. In one of them he refers to the variety of architectural detail in Venice, adding that '... the pencil of Canaletti conveys so perfect an idea as to render all verbal description superfluous'. (Before the nineteenth century the word 'pencil' was applied to any painter's brush.) We know nothing of the Canalettos he had in mind: all that we know is that in 1787 Beckford employed Sir John Soane to build a picture gallery for him and that in 1807 he sold Fonthill Splendens and its contents in a sale at Phillips's auction rooms which lasted for seven days. Lot 605 in that sale was the *Riva*, described as a 'View of Venice (from the Calonne collection). A most capital performance of this great master CANALETTI'. Sir John paid 150 guineas for it and hung it first at his official residence at Chelsea Hospital, where he was Clerk of Works from March 1807 until his death. In 1812 Soane rebuilt No. 13 Lincoln's Inn Fields as his private residence, moving out of his previous home, the next-door house at No. 12, which he had rebuilt in 1792–4. No. 12 was rented out from 1813 but in 1819 Soane took

FIG.11 Canaletto, *The Bacino di S. Marco, looking East*, probably early 1730s. Oil on canvas, 125 × 153 cm (49 1/8 × 80 1/2 in). Boston, Museum of Fine Arts, Abbott Lawrence Fund, Seth K. Sweetser Fund, and Charles Edward French Fund (no.39.290).

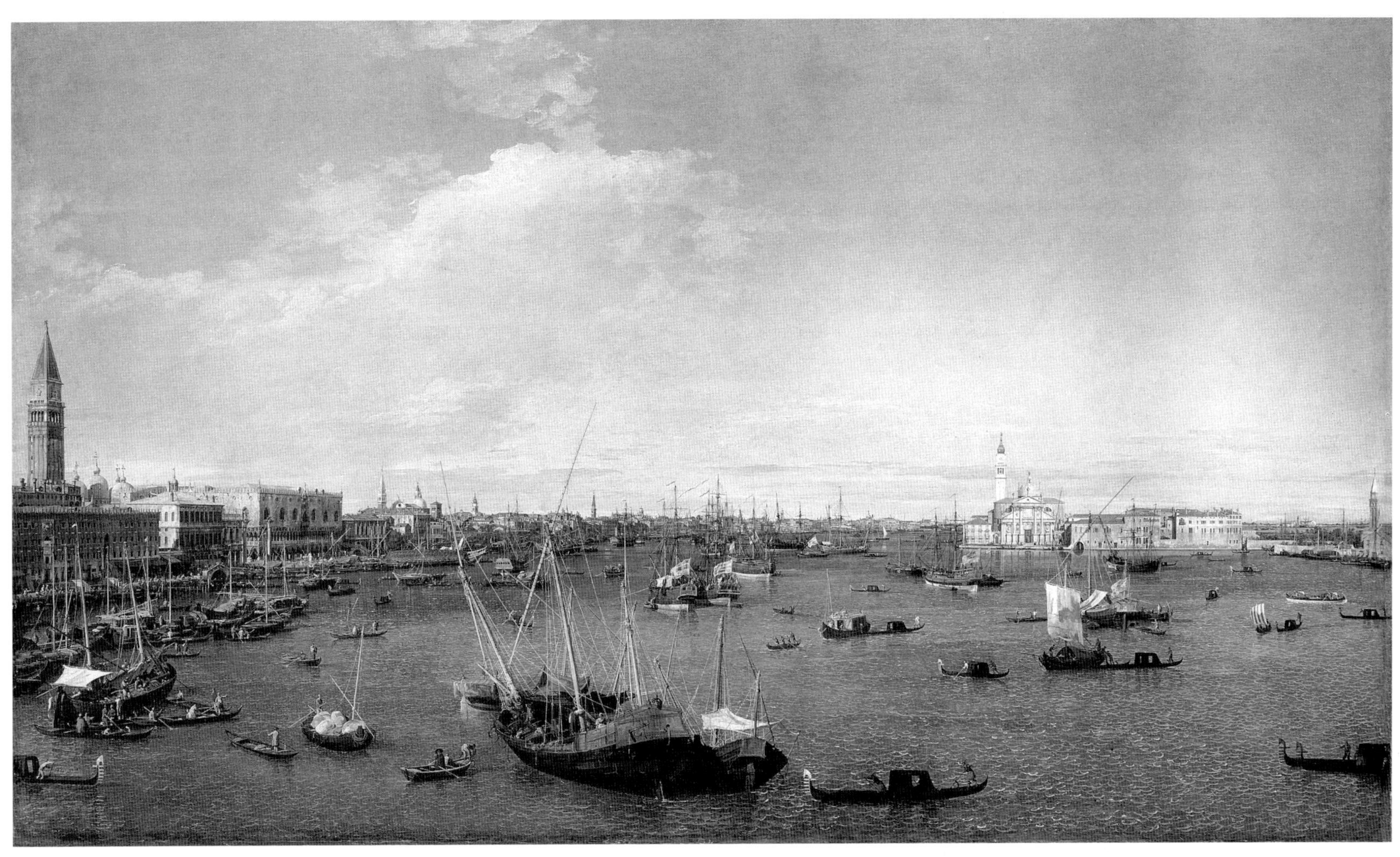

advantage of a renewal of the lease to take over for his own use a ground-floor room at the back of the house, opening a door through into his adjacent Museum at No. 13 and redesigning the room to form his first Picture Gallery. The *Riva* hung in this room from 1819 to 1825. In October 1823, Soane was able to buy and rebuild No. 14 Lincoln's Inn Fields. At the back of the site he built a new Picture Room in which, from 1825, the *Riva* was hung above the fireplace, occupying the prime position in the room, surrounded by Soane's celebrated Hogarths and architectural drawings. Once this room was in use Soane's first picture gallery was blocked off once more from his main residence at No. 13 and leased out with the rest of No. 12. The lease of No. 12 expired in 1889 and James Wild, the curator of what by then was the museum, took the space back as part of it. He rebuilt Soane's first Picture Room as his 'New Picture Room' and hung all three Canalettos there for the benefit of art students wishing to copy them. This is where they still hang. The invitation to students may well account for some of the copies of the *Riva* painting which have reached the market despite the fact that no engraving of it was ever published. This does not apply to the version owned by the Kress Foundation, now in the Seattle Art Museum after some years at the National Gallery, Washington. The Kress picture appears to be a replica of the Soane painting and to have originated in Canaletto's studio at the time the original was still available. A number of such replicas of Canaletto's work exist and all that can safely be said of them is that their purpose and their relationship to Canaletto himself are far from clear and are still being studied.

By 1991–2 all three paintings by Canaletto at the Soane Museum were badly in need of cleaning and restoration, and this was carried out by Viola Pemberton-Pigott. Only then could their high quality be appreciated by a later generation; but it was perhaps not until 1994–5, when the Riva was exhibited in *The Glory of Venice* exhibition at the Royal Academy in London (no. 139), that it became recognized as one of the handful of masterpieces painted by Canaletto in the 1730s.

Facing page, detail of PL.1.

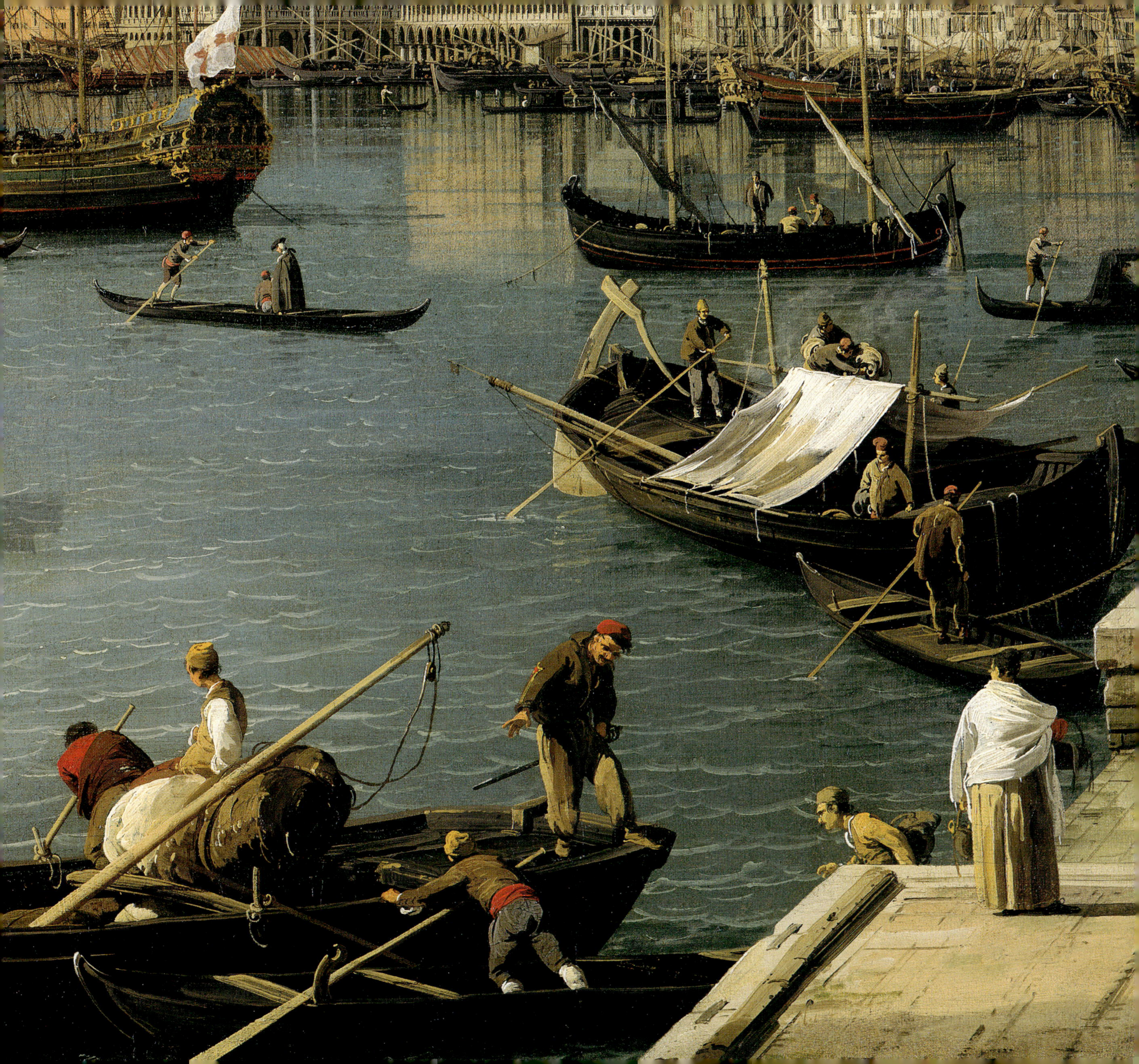

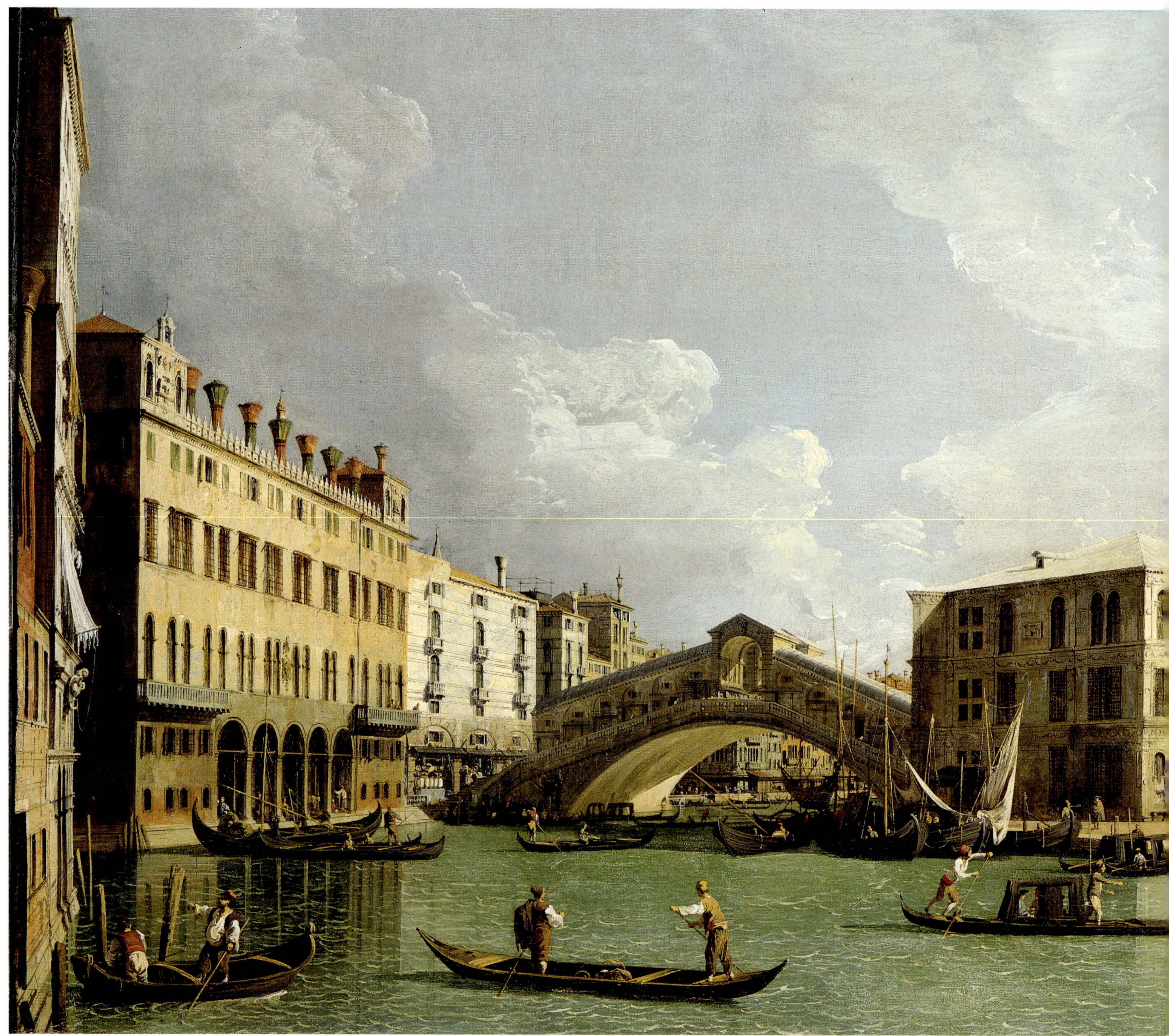

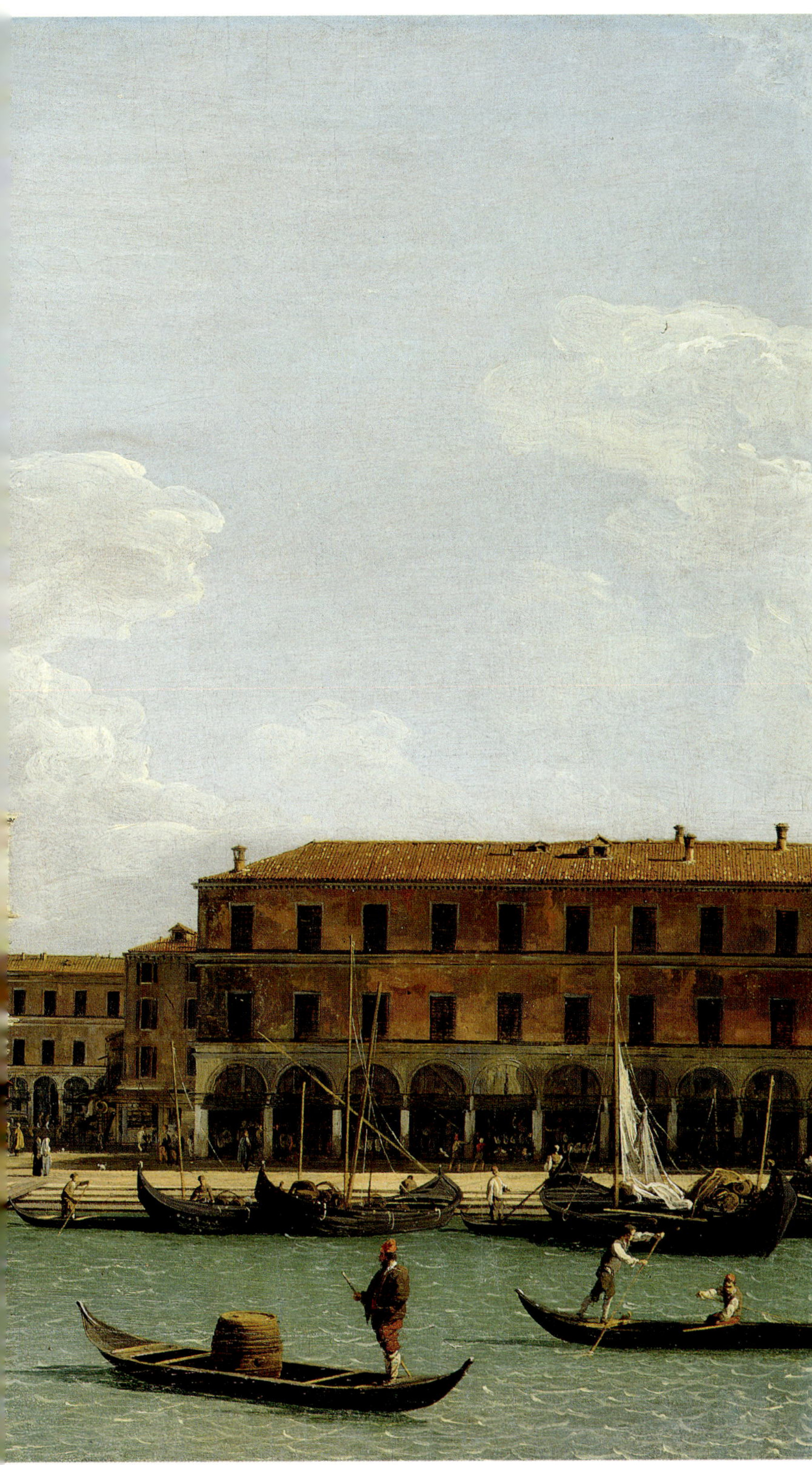

PL.2 Canaletto, *The Rialto Bridge from the North*, c. 1734–5. Oil on canvas, 64.1 × 109.7 cm (25 1/4 × 43 3/16). London, Sir John Soane's Museum (no.P61).

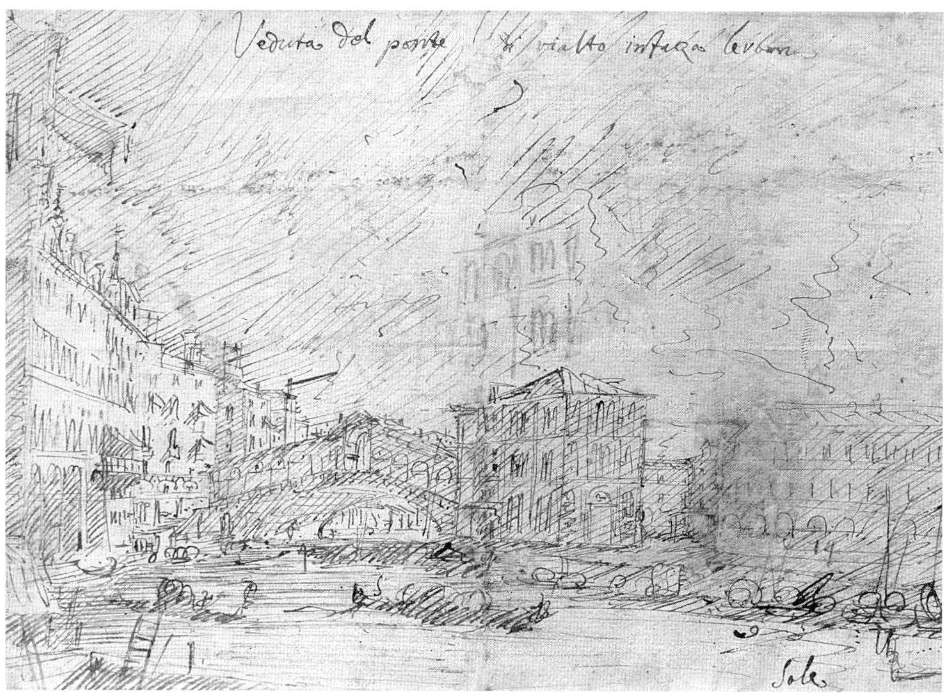

FIG.12 Canaletto, *The Rialto Bridge from the North*, 1725. Pen and brown paper, 14.1 × 20.2 cm (5 1/2 × 8 in). Oxford, Ashmolean Museum (no.P11975).
The word *sole* shows where Canaletto intended to show the sun striking the water. The drawing is closely related to Stefano Conti's painting of the scene (FIG.13), as is established by the existence of a companion drawing which contains features existing only in the pair to this picture, the Conti version of the view looking north from the bridge. It is a preparatory drawing for the painting, therefore, but it could hardly have been made on the site given its various viewpoints.

The Rialto Bridge from the North

Oil on canvas, 64.1 × 109.7cm (25 1/4 × 43 3/16), c. 1734–5

The painting shows the first of the celebrated monuments to greet the ordinary visitor on his way into Venice (PL.2). Although princes, and others whom Venice needed to impress, were greeted as they disembarked at the Doge's Palace, the great majority of travellers entered by gondola or post boat at Mestre or Fusina, crossed the lagoon and entered the Grand Canal from the Cannaregio or S. Chiara. Only when at last they reached the Rialto Bridge did they become aware of the wonders that awaited them.

Most of them would agree that this beautifully composed and harmonious picture faithfully recorded what they had seen, but this is far from the case. The reader interested in studying how Canaletto has manoeuvred the component buildings would do well to refer to the aerial views, one oblique (FIG.15) and one from overhead (FIG.16) showing the positions they really occupy.

At first sight the chosen viewpoint is from a boat moored alongside the Palazzo Civran (at the bottom of the aerial views). This, though, is merely to provide a repoussoir effect, to push the picture back: scarcely anything of interest could be seen looking straight ahead from here. Canaletto therefore moves across the Grand Canal to a point from which the huge Fondaco dei Tedeschi can be properly seen (on the left). Now the Post Office, this was originally given to German traders for their warehouse. In 1505

Facing page
FIG.13 Canaletto, *The Rialto Bridge from the North*, 1725. Oil on canvas, 91.5 × 134.5 cm (36 × 53 in). Canada, private collection.
This is Canaletto's earliest version of the scene, painted in 1725 for Stefano Conti.

FIG.14 Canaletto, *The Rialto Bridge from the North*, late 1720s. Oil on canvas, 47 × 80 cm (18 1/2 × 31 1/2 in). H.M. The Queen, Windsor Castle (no.ML390.WC317).
This was Joseph Smith's own version of the scene, engraved by Visentini. This painting remained in Smith's hands until his collection was sold to George III. Painted in the late 1720s, after Conti's and the Duke of Richmond's versions (FIGS 13 and 4) but before Sir John Soane's.

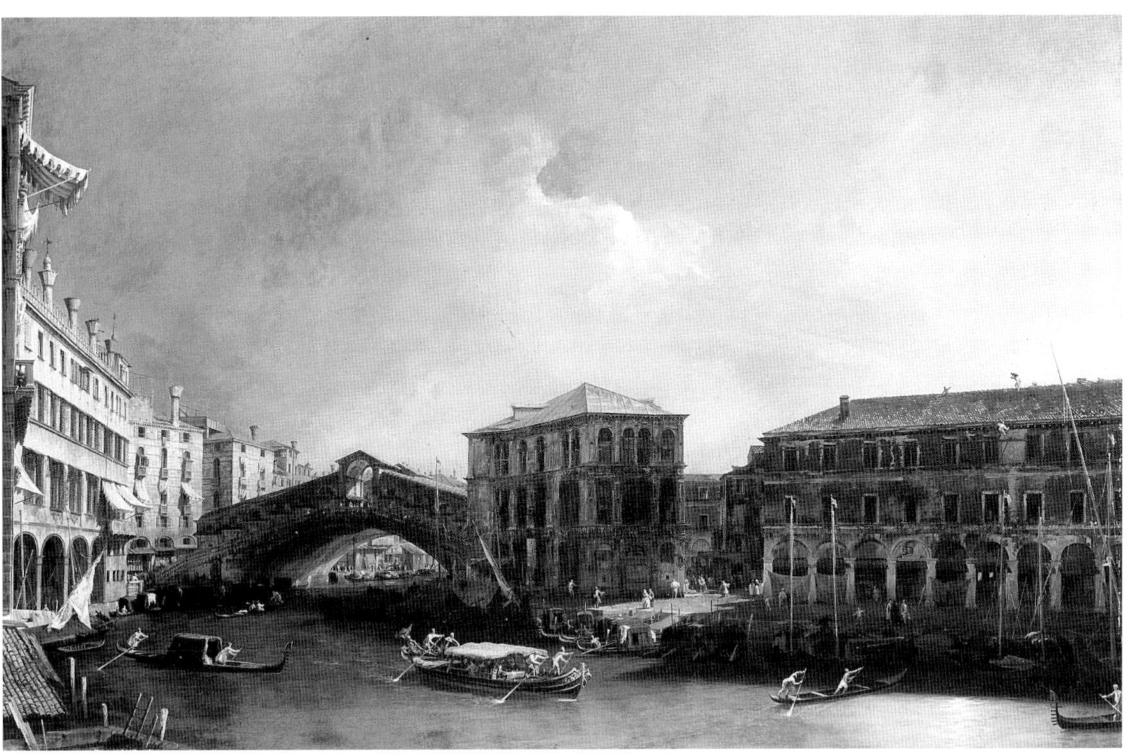

13

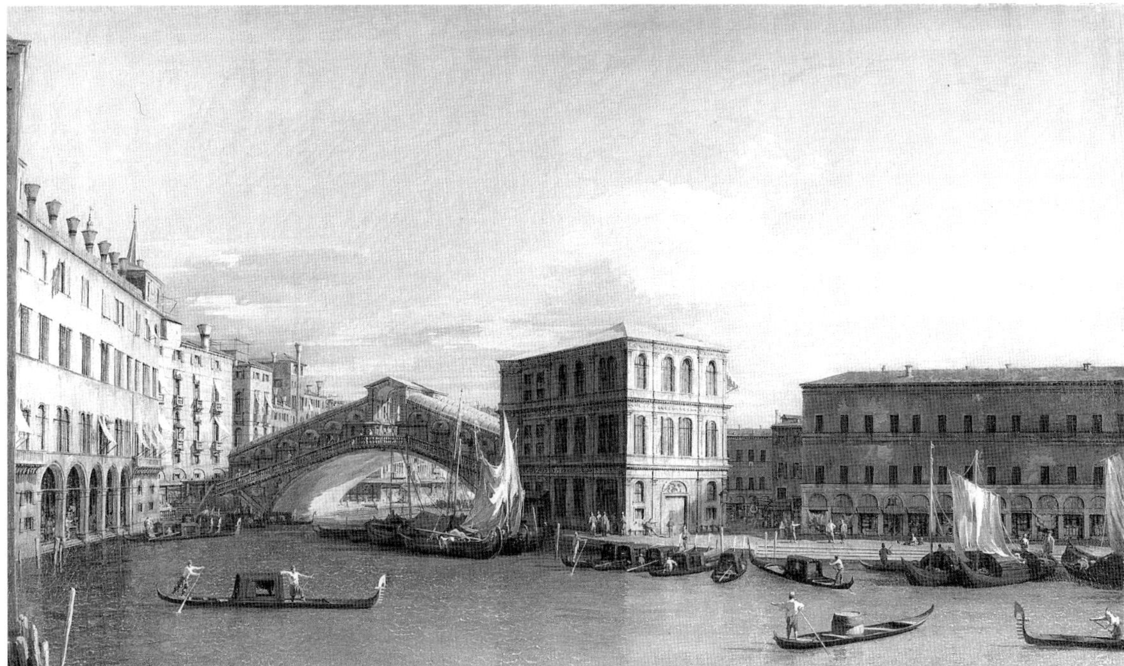

14

it was burnt down and when rebuilt the Grand Canal façade was frescoed by Giorgione and that on the south side by Titian.[10] In Canaletto's time traces of these frescoes remained and twirls of reddish paint are visible which can only be intended to indicate them. (To Ruskin, a century later, they were 'flaming like the reflection of a sunset'.) From the same position it was possible for Canaletto to see under the Rialto Bridge and we are given a glimpse of the busy *fondamenta* beyond it. But it was a wholly unsuitable viewpoint for the right-hand half of the picture looking, as it did, on to a wall of the unusual five-sided Palazzo dei Camerlenghi. Canaletto therefore moves with the curve of the canal to a point from which two façades of that palace can be seen together with the old buildings (Fabbriche Vecchie) of the vegetable market, with another glimpse between the two of a busy street which in fact leads to the Rialto Bridge and which he makes far closer than it really is.

This subtle and complex composition had been worked out long before as can be seen from the existence of a preparatory drawing (FIG.12), Stefano Conti's painting of 1725 (FIG.13) and one of the Duke of Richmond's pair later on (FIG.4). Only the building fractionally shown on the extreme left and, more importantly, the angle of the Fondaco dei Tedeschi, varied. By about 1730, when the subject became one of Smith's twelve Grand Canal paintings, the change of style brought about by McSwiney had matured but the figures in Smith's version (FIG.14) are lifeless compared with those of the somewhat later Soane picture. There is no trace here of the perfunctoriness which sometimes crept into work of the early 1730s and inevitably into later versions. The figures are full of life, the architecture painted with great detail, as are the rigging and sails of the craft. A glance at the merchandise visible through the arcade on the right leaves no doubt that Canaletto's brush was assured and his interest in the subject fully maintained, familiar though it was.

The Piazza S. Marco, looking South-West

Oil on canvas, 70.2 × 114.6 cm (27 5/8 × 45 1/8 in), c.1734–5

Topographical artists have always delighted in depicting on their paper or canvas more than would be visible in the thirty- or forty-degree angle of vision perceived by the human eye looking straight ahead. A slight movement of the eye or head will enable the artist to encompass a wider angle: too much will produce distortion when recorded which must be corrected at risk of loss of conviction. To move the viewpoint further away will change the relationship of the component parts. Some artists, notably Carlevaris who was working when Canaletto was still a child, would choose an imaginary viewpoint so far away as to produce an 'impossible' view. Canaletto himself made a small group of drawings (of which FIG.17 is one) purporting to be able to see an angle of 180 degrees, a full semicircle. The result is often disturbing and

Facing page, detail of PL.2.

FIG.15 Oblique aerial photograph of the Grand Canal, north of the Rialto Bridge. On the right are part of the Fabbriche Vecchie (old buildings) and Fabbriche Nuove (new buildings), with the vegetable market. The five-sided building to their left is the Palazzo Camerlenghi, followed by the bridge. The left foreground buildings, of which only parts are seen, are (from the bridge) the Fondaco dei Tedeschi, two rebuilt houses and the Palazzo Civran, Canaletto's purported viewpoint.

FIG.16 Overhead aerial photograph showing the true relationship of the Rialto Bridge to the surrounding buildings.

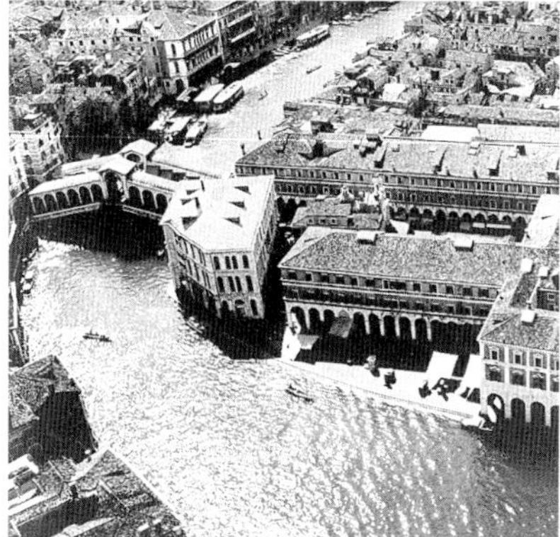

15

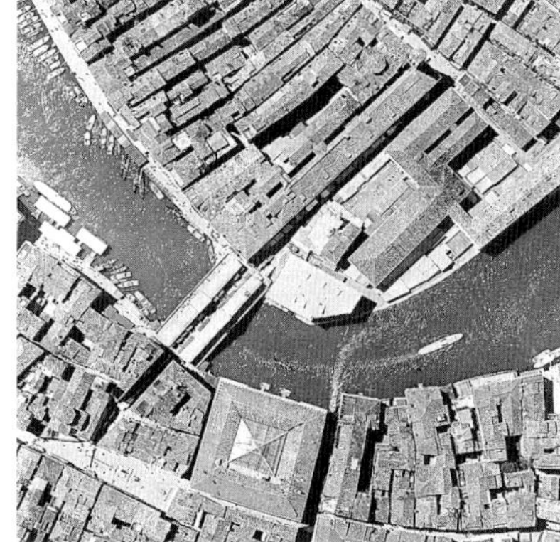

16

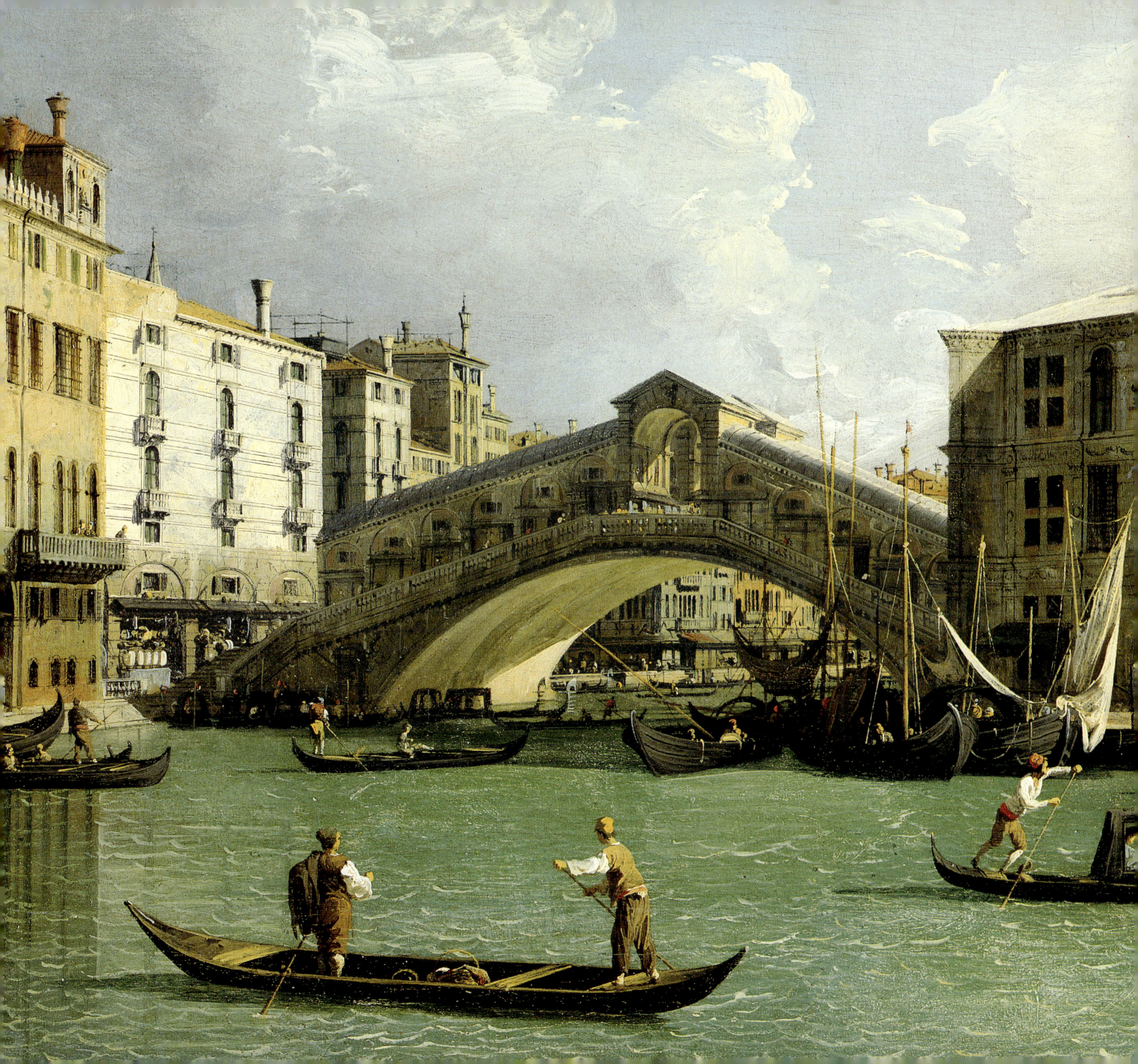

PL.3 Canaletto, *The Piazza S. Marco looking South-West*, c. 1734–5. Oil on canvas, 70.2 × 114.6cm (27 5/8 × 45 1/8 in). London, Sir John Soane's Museum (no.P63).

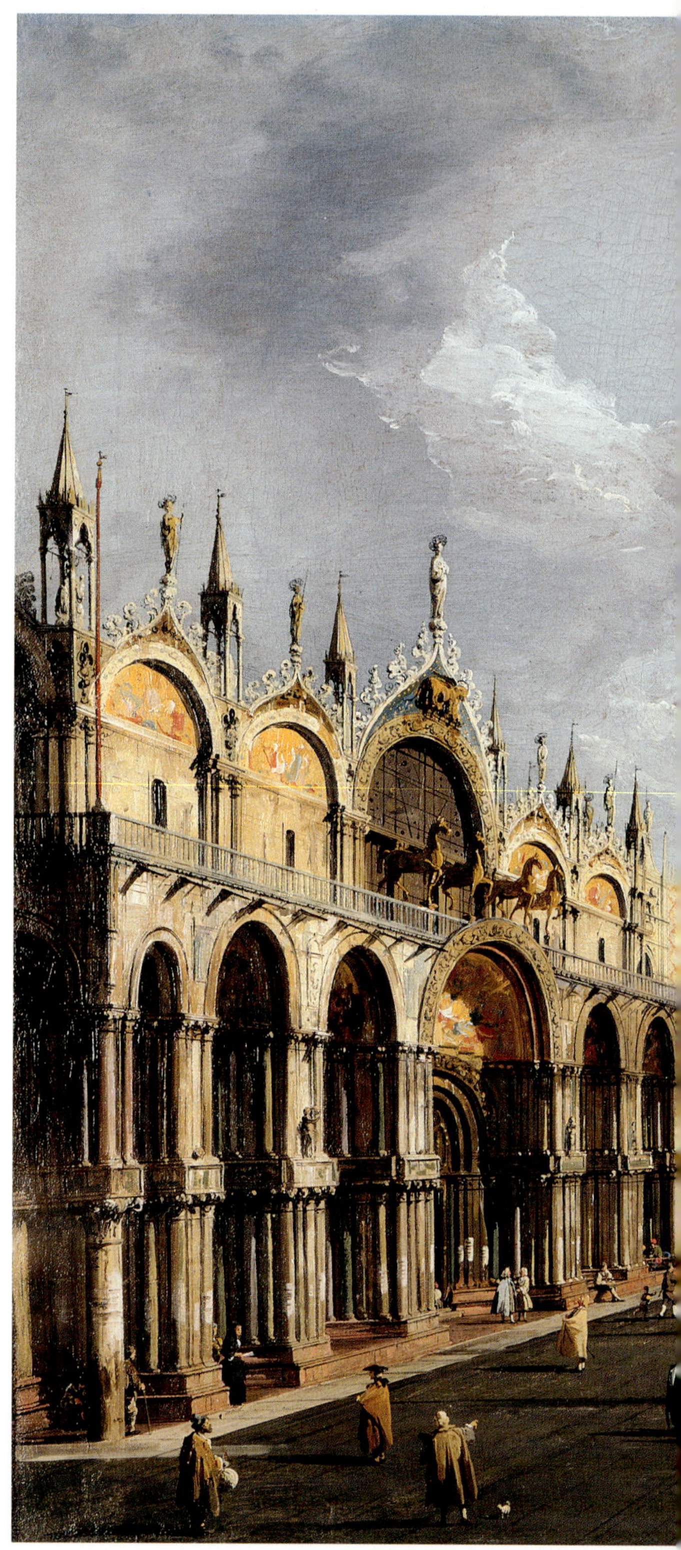

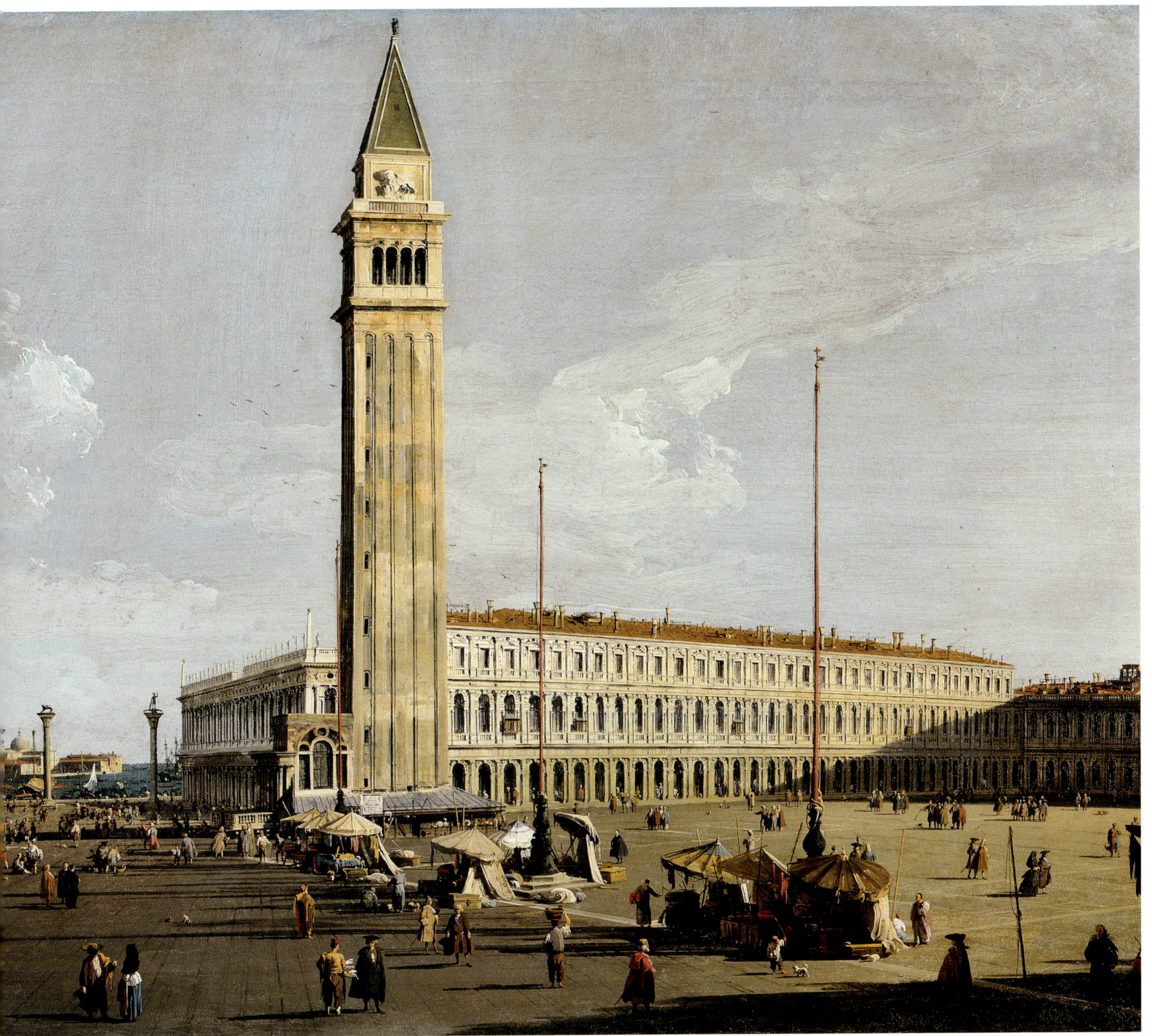

displeasing. However, as we have seen in *The Rialto Bridge from the North*, his practice of using two or more viewpoints at a normal distance from his subject was exercised with such skill that it often went unnoticed and the viewer was left with an impression of photographic accuracy.

In Canaletto's lifetime and ever since, it has often been suggested that the camera obscura played an important role in his work. A camera obscura is the equivalent of a modern camera except that the image is projected on to a screen or white surface instead of a film and the viewer must be in the dark to see it. Canaletto never hesitated to use instruments such as rulers and dividers and would certainly have used optical instruments had he found them helpful. In the case of the 'impossible' views, and many wide-angle pictures, the camera obscura could have played no part at all: there was nowhere from which such a view could be projected.

Canaletto must have been familiar with the 1703 engravings of Carlevaris which included the one reproduced in FIG.18. It is more of a diagram than a work of art but Canaletto chose much the same purported viewpoint, although far lower, for a painting which must have been among his very first views of Venice in the early 1720s. He was already prepared to deceive the eye by showing the whole of the Campanile whereas only the lower part would be visible from the assumed distance unless the viewer raised his head. But he could not pretend, as Carlevaris had pretended, that the western end of the Piazza could be seen so he included only a few bays of the south side.

Ten years later Canaletto made a drawing which he inscribed *Anno–1731* (FIG.19). It was in poor condition when it was recently discovered but it is closely related to, if not the preparatory drawing for, the Soane *Piazza*, which was probably painted three or four years later. The viewpoint has been moved to the left and is lower and closer to the lagoon, so that the façade of Sansovino's Library (to the left of the Campanile) becomes visible and the viewer now has the flagstaffs on his right instead of intrusively before his eyes.

But neither drawing nor painting was ever intended to be a conventional view from, say, a window in the Clocktower. Canaletto now turns his head and shows the scene looking west instead of south. He adds realism by foreshortening the buildings onthe south side of the piazza, the Procuratie Nuove, which Carlevaris made no pretence of doing, but he cuts the right side of his picture abruptly before the façade of S. Geminiano is complete.

The viewpoint of the right side of the Soane picture remains uncertain until comparison is made with another version, not quite as high but wider, now in Hartford, Connecticut, but with no known history (FIG.21). The viewpoint of the Hartford painting is to the right (west) of that of the Soane painting. It includes the north side of the piazza (in the right foreground), steeply foreshortened and in deep shadow, but unmistakable, and the whole of the S. Geminiano end. As if to recognize that there

FIG.17 Canaletto, *The Piazza S. Marco, looking South-West*, c. 1730–35. Pen and brown ink over pencil, some lines ruled, 18.2 × 37.7 cm (7¼ × 14⅞ in). H.M. The Queen, Windsor Castle (no.RL7422). This drawing is close to the Soane painting except that the south side of the Piazza is not foreshortened and almost the whole of the west side is shown. Probably drawn after the painting and then given or sold to Smith.

FIG.18 Luca Carlevaris, *Altre Veduta della Piazza di S. Marco*, No.43 of 104 etchings in Sir John Soane's copy of *Le Fabriche e vedute di Venezia Disegnate, Poste in Prospettiva, et Intagliate da Luca Carlevaris*. London, Sir John Soane's Museum.

FIG.19 Canaletto, *The Piazza S. Marco, looking South-West*, unknown date. Pen and ink, now oxidized, 25 × 40.2 cm (9¾ × 15¾ in). Whereabouts unknown. Closer to the Soane painting than FIG.17.

FIG.20 Here attributed to Canaletto, 1730s. Otherwise attributed to Bernardo Bellotto, *The Piazza S. Marco, looking South-West*, c. 1740. Oil on canvas, 136.2 × 232.5 cm (53⅝ × 9¹¹⁄₁₂ in). The Cleveland Museum of Art, 1997, Leonard C. Hanna, Jr., Fund (no.1962.169).

FIG.21 Canaletto, *The Piazza S. Marco, looking South-West*, between 1731 and 1740, probably c. 1740. Oil on canvas, 67.3 × 102.8 cm (26½ × 40½ in). Hartford, Connecticut, The Wadsworth Atheneum (no.1947.2).

FIG.22 Canaletto, *Piazza S. Marco, looking South and West*, 1730s. Oil on canvas, 45 × 75 cm (17¾ × 29½ in). Udine, Italy. Private Collection Maron Di Brugnera.

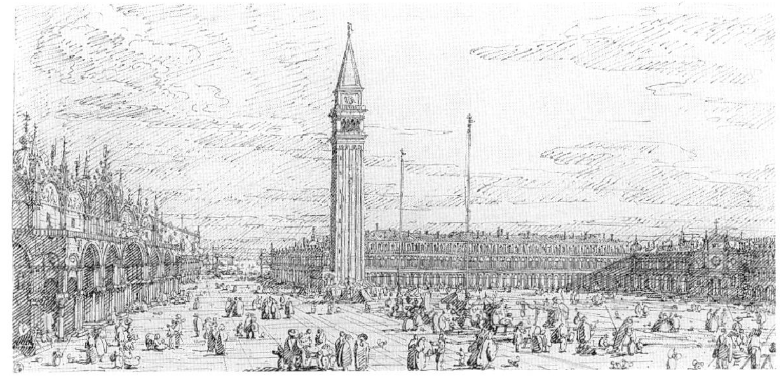

17

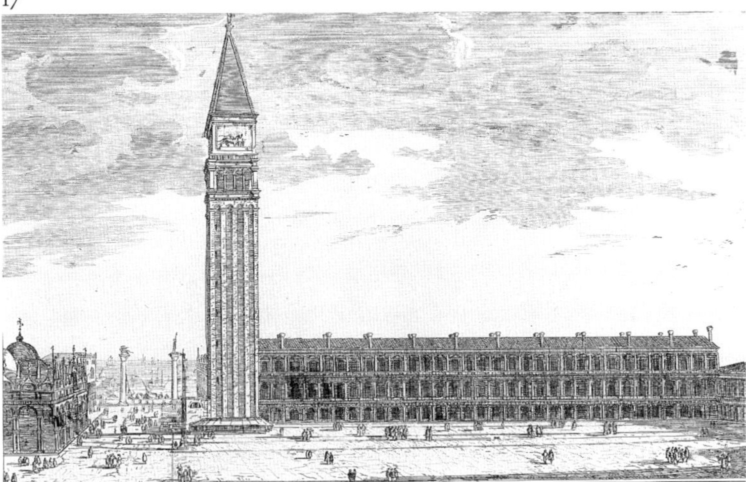

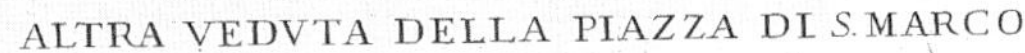

18

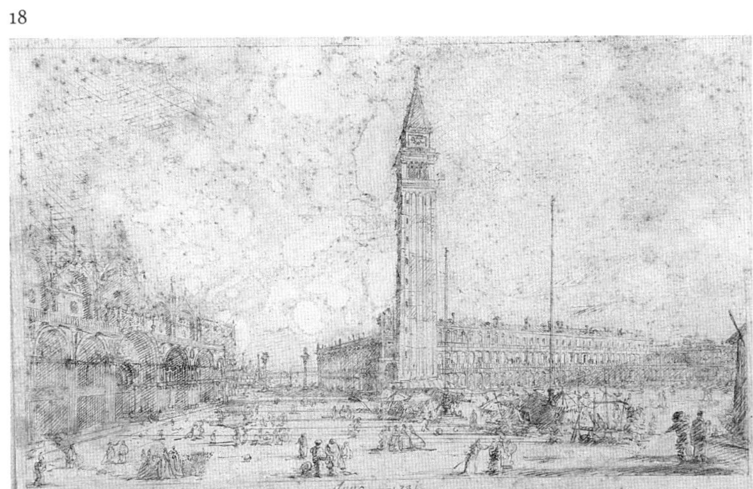

19

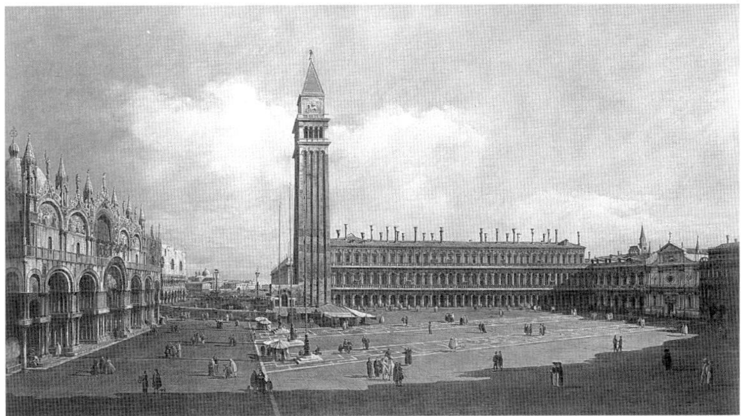

20

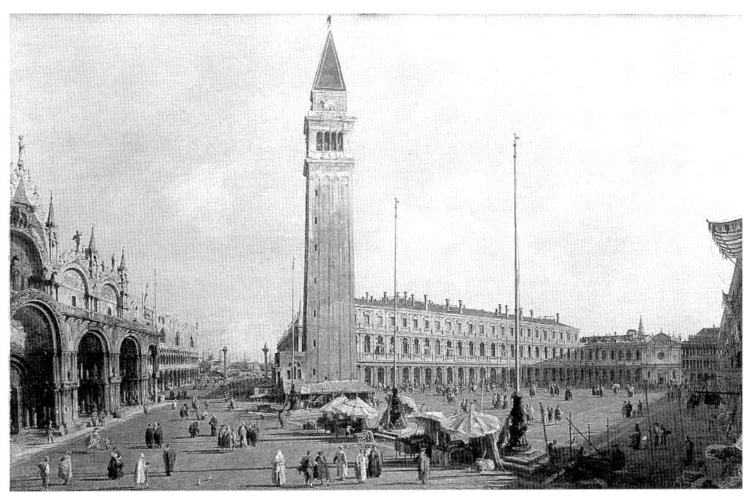

21

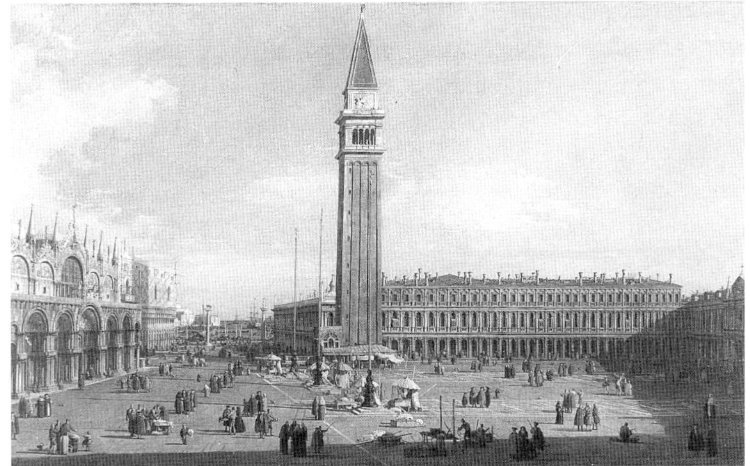

22

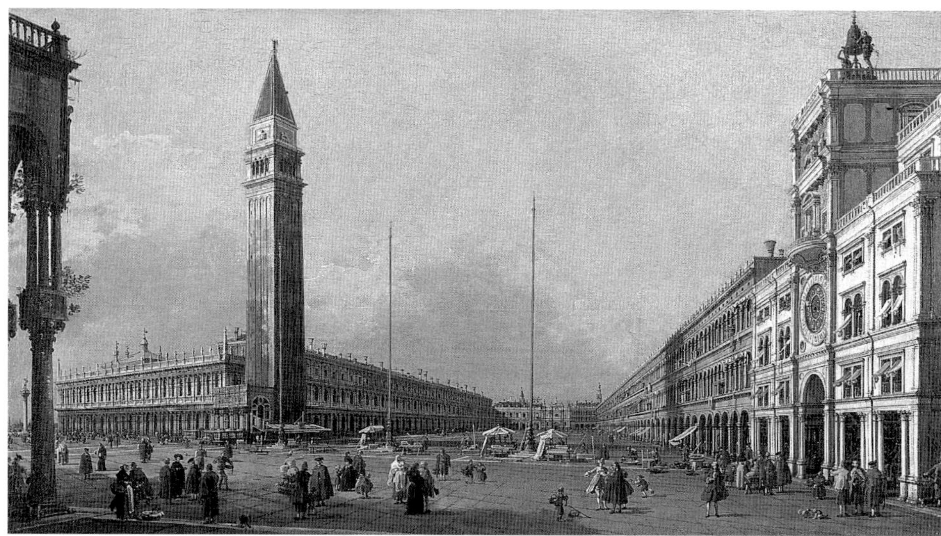

FIG.23 Canaletto, *The Piazza S. Marco, looking South and West*, 1763. Oil on canvas, 59.1 × 102.8 cm (22¹/₄ × 40¹/₄ in). Los Angeles County Museum of Art, Gift of the Ahmanson Foundation (no.M.83.39).
Signed 'Io Antonio Canal, detto il Canaletto (*sic*), fecit 1763' on the verso of the canvas. In this, his last view painting, Canaletto shows complete mastery of the 'impossible' view. On the left is the northernmost column of St Mark's, with foliage perhaps suggesting the capricious nature of the view, then, after a glimpse of the Lagoon, the whole of the Piazzetta and Piazza including, extreme right, the Clocktower with its alterations of 1755. The brilliant composition, in a way embodying the artist's lifework, together with the inscription, suggest that the picture may have been intended as Canaletto's reception piece for the Academy to which he had been elected in 1763.

Facing page, detail of PL.3.

is a limit to an acceptable angle of vision, the northern part of S. Marco has been omitted in compensation.

As Canaletto must have realised, the success or failure of this daring composition depended much on the way the two sides were fused together by the depiction of the Campanile. The need to show it in its entirety, abandoning reality, now becomes apparent and in the Hartford version a touch of realism is added by showing it narrowing as it ascends thus giving it its familiar dumpy appearance. Characteristically, Canaletto has reduced the number of windows of the Procuratie Nuove, behind the Campanile, by a third, believing, no doubt, that the building would look better that way.

Although the composition of the Hartford painting is more satisfactory, and the closer viewpoint shows the market stalls in more detail, the figures lack the liveliness of those in the earlier Soane version. This combination of fantasy and reality seems nevertheless to have been well received. Several versions followed including a huge one (233 cm wide) probably dating from the early 1740s when Bellotto's presence in the studio was at its most apparent (FIG.22). Some of these, like FIG.20, have been firmly attributed to Bellotto and a number (like FIGS 20 and 22) seem to be closely derived from Carlevaris's etching (FIG.18). Smith, too, owned a drawing which does not seem to be related to any known painting so that others, as yet unknown, may have existed.

More than twenty years later, in a painting signed and dated 1763 (FIG.23), Canaletto reached the culmination of his desire to show the viewer more than his own eyes could see. He had just been elected to the Academy of Fine Art and must

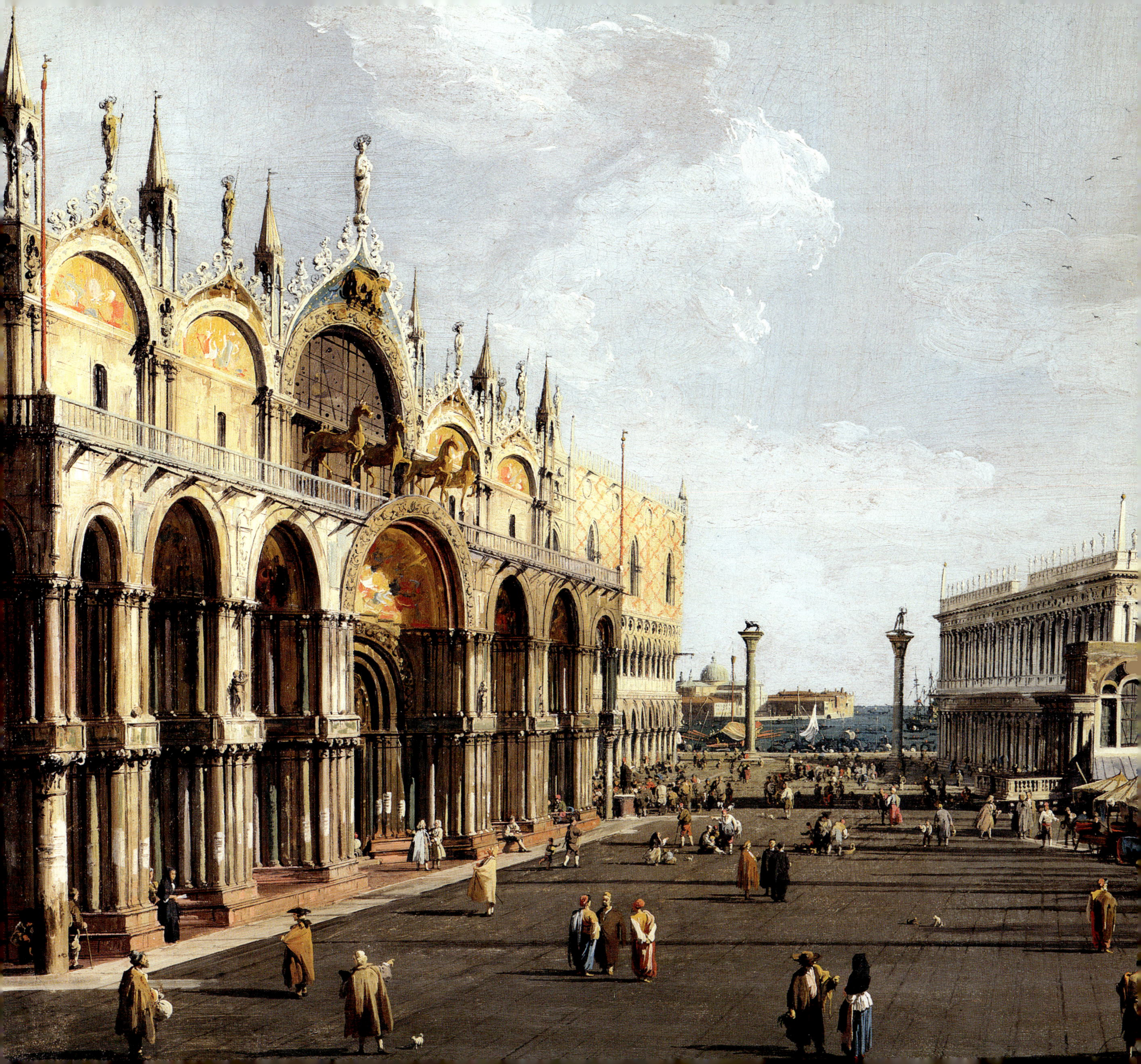

surely have intended this, his last picture of the Piazza, as his reception piece to sum up his long career. But the Academicians were apparently not yet ready to accept view painting as fine art. Canaletto kept them waiting for two years and then gave them an architectural capriccio which pleased them more.

History

The *Rialto Bridge* and the *Piazza S. Marco* paintings were bought for Sir John Soane on 19 March 1796 at the sale by Christie's of the 3rd Earl of Bute's collection from Highcliffe, Hampshire. Bute had died in 1792 and the sale, which followed the demolition of the house, contained only a small part of his vast collection.

Joseph Farington recorded in his diary on the day before that the pictures were 'chiefly sea pieces & very bad, the collection having been gleaned by Genl. Stuart. Three Canalettis good pictures'.[11] Soane's Note Book records that on the day of the sale he set off at 6 a.m. for Buckinghamshire, where he was building a house, which explains why Farington's entry for that day reads, 'Ld Bute's, sale of his High Cliff pictures, I went to. Mrs Soane gave 36 guineas for a Canaletti & 35 guineas for its companion.' The pictures were described simply as views in Venice and the price was low, bearing in mind their size. Francis Russell has pointed out, though, that many major pictures were arriving in London as a result of the French Revolution and other extensive collections were being sold.[12] Moreover, the fact that Charles Stuart, Bute's favourite son, was known to have 'gleaned' (taken for himself) the best pictures would have deterred many important buyers.

Bute, at one time Prime Minister, was much involved in the purchase by his friend, George III, of Smith's collection in 1763 and he did, in the last years of Smith's life, buy books from him. His younger brother, the British envoy to Turin, was in correspondence with Smith from 1743. The presence of a drawing in Smith's collection, closer to the Soane *Piazza S. Marco* than to any other version (FIG.17) makes it tempting to suggest that the painting might have passed through Smith's hands. The same suggestion has been made about the Vienna *Riva*, also on the grounds that Smith owned a drawing of the subject (see p.26 above). Although there is no evidence that Bute bought any of his pictures from Smith there is always the possibility that Smith might have sold the painting to an earlier buyer. Nor is there any evidence as to when the two pictures were brought together. They are not subjects which would be paired together naturally. The subject of *The Rialto Bridge from the North* is often paired with another painting of the Rialto Bridge and the *Piazza S. Marco* painting stands on its own. Christie's, it will be noted, did not sell them as a pair in the Bute sale.

Notes

1. Well known as these splendid early paintings are through reproduction, it is to Dresden, or the galleries of private collectors that we must turn for the originals (until two of them returned to Venice in the 1980s, there were none left in Canaletto's native city).
2. John Russell, reviewing the New York Canaletto exhibition in the *New York Times Art Review*, November, 1989.
3. G.A. Guarienti in Orlandi's *Abecedario pittorico*, 1753, p. 75.
4. The only evidence that he was successful before Smith's advent came from those who wanted their clients so to believe, including, of course, McSwiney and Smith themselves.
5. Charles de Brosses, *Lettres familières ...*, 24 November 1739.
6. Pietro Edwards, letter in the archives of the Seminario Patriarcel, quoted by Francis Haskell, 'Francesco Guardi as *Vedutista*', *Journal of the Warburg and Courtauld Institutes*, 1960, pp.256–7
7. Gianpietro Zuchetti, *Venezia, Ponte per ponte*, Venice, 1993, p. 324.
8. For Schulenburg, see F. Haskell, *Patrons and Painters*, 1963, p. 310ff.
9. For Schulenburg's catalogue and accounts see Alice Binion, *La Galleria scomparsa del ... Schulenburg*, Milan, 1990, and p. 29 of her essay on *Schulenburg's Bellottos* in the catalogue of the Bellotto exhibition at Castelvecchio, Verona, 1990, in which she first published the identification.
10. I am indebted to Professor Jaynie Anderson for this piece of recent scholarship. It used to be thought that both façades were frescoed by Giorgione.
11. *The Farington Diary*, 1793–1817, edited by J. Grigg, London, 1922.
12. 'Engagements at Sea', by Francis Russell, *Country Life*, 26 January 1984, p. 227.

Concordances

The concordance is with the standard *catalogue raisonné* of Canaletto's works by W.G. Constable, *Canaletto*, 1962, revised by J.G. Links in 1976 and 1989 (denoted by C/L).

Concordance by plate/figure number

PL.1	C/L122
PL.2	C/L236n
PL.3	C/L54n
FIG.3	C/L335
FIG.4	C/L235
FIG.5	C/L112
FIG.8	C/L575
FIG.9	C/L577
FIG.10	C/L121
FIG.11	C/L133
FIG.12	C/L593
FIG.13	C/L234
FIG .14	C/L236
FIG.17	C/L537
FIG.19	C/L537*
FIG.20	C/L53
FIG .21	C/L54
FIG.22	C/L53*
FIG.23	C/L54*

Concordance by *catalogue raisonné* number

C/L53	FIG. 20
C/L53*	FIG. 22
C/L54	FIG.21
C/L54n	PL.3
C/L54*	FIG.23
C/L112	FIG.5
C/L121	FIG.10
C/L122	PL.1
C/L133	FIG.11
C/L234	FIG. 13
C/L235	FIG.4
C/L236	FIG. 14
C/L236n	PL.2
C/L335	FIG.3
C/L537	FIG.17
C/L537*	FIG.19
C/L575	FIG.8
C/L577	FIG.9
C/L593	FIG.12

Bibliography

Sources for all statements concerning Canaletto, his associates and his work, will be found in *Canaletto* by W.G. Constable, revised by J.G. Links, Oxford, 1989, with later supplement; or in *Canaletto*, the catalogue of the exhibition held at the Metropolitan Museum of Art, New York, 1989–90, by Katharine Baetjer and J.G. Links.

Other standard works on the subject include *The Later Italian Painters*, by Michael Levey (London, 1971); *Canaletto, Paintings and Drawings* by Oliver Millar (London, 1980–81); *Canaletto Drawings at Windsor Castle* by K.T. Parker (1st edition, Oxford, 1948) with an appendix by Charlotte Crawley (Bologna, 1990); *The Later Italian Pictures* (of the Royal Collection) by Michael Levey (1st edition, Oxford, 1964; 2nd edition, Cambridge, 1991); and *Canaletto*, the catalogue of an exhibition held at Venice, edited by Alessandro Bettagno (Vicenza, 1992).

For a short history of eighteenth-century Venice see the final chapters of *Venice: the Greatness and the Fall* by John Julius Norwich (London, 1981), and the catalogue for the exhibition *The Glory of Venice: Art in the 18th Century* (London, 1992). The latest work on Visentini is the catalogue of the exhibition *Canaletto & Visentini* by Dario Succi (Venice, 1986), and on Joseph Smith *The Consul Smith Collection* by Frances Vivian (Munich, 1989) and the catalogue of an exhibition held at the Queen's Gallery, *A King's Purchase* (with bibliography; London, 1993). Frances Vivian's *Il Console Smith* (Vicenza, 1971) remains the only biography. For Schulenberg, see *La Galleria scomparsi del ... Schulenberg* by Alice Binion (Milan, 1990). Finally, *Canaletto and his Patrons* by J.G. Links (London, 1977) contains a select bibliography on the use of the camera obscura (pp. 107–8).

Acknowledgements

All research on the history of the pictures was carried out by Helen Dorey, Deputy Curator, Sir John Soane's Museum, with the exception of the Schulenburg association which was researched by Professor Alice Binion. I am also deeply indebted to Helen Dorey for her editorship of this publication.

Photographic credits

PLS 1–3 and FIG.18: © The Trustees of Sir John Soane's Museum; FIG.4: By Courtesy of the Goodwood Trustees: photograph Courtauld Institute of Art; FIG.5: By courtesy of the Trustees of the Wallace Collection; FIGS 6 and 7: J.G. Links; FIGS 9, 14 and 17: The Royal Collection © Her Majesty The Queen; FIG.10: Kunsthistorisches Museum, Vienna; FIG.11: Courtesy, Museum of Fine Arts, Boston; FIG.12: By courtesy of the Visitors of the Ashmolean Museum, Oxford; FIG.13: Courtesy Art Gallery of Ontario; FIG.20: © The Cleveland Museum of Art, 1997, Leonard C. Hanna. Jr., Fund. 1962.169; FIG.21: The Wadsworth Atheneum, Hartford. The Ella Gallup Sumner and Mary Caitlin Sumner Collection Fund. Endowed by Mr. and Mrs. Thomas R Cox, Jr.; FIG.23: copyright © 1997 Museum Associates, Los Angeles County Museum of Art, Gift of the Ahmanson Foundation.